# WHAT'S WORTH FIGHTING FOR?

## Michael Fullan and Andy Hargreaves

### What's Worth Fighting For in Your School?

Schools have failed to capitalize on the strengths of people and to forge collaborative relationships within the school. Encouraging teachers and principals to
think more deeply about school reform, individual responsibility, and collaborative culture, *What's Worth Fighting For in Your School?* provides exciting ideas
and methods for teachers and principals to act as moral change agents and help
fight to establish new, more powerful working and learning conditions in their
profession.

### What's Worth Fighting For "Out There"?

*What's Worth Fighting For "Out There"?* shows why we need to broaden the
commitment to collaboration and community beyond the walls of the
school. In a world of growing complexity, rapid change and transparent
boundaries, if we are to bring about significant improvements in
teaching and learning within schools we must develop strong, open
connections beyond schools—with parents, communities, businesses,
universities, learning networks. Teachers and principals must go wider
and deeper if substantial reform is to be achieved. This book provides
specific ideas and guidelines for action for teachers and principals to
build such multifaceted relationships.

### What's Worth Fighting For in Leadership for Change?

Using the previous two books as a foundation, this third book in the
trilogy redefines leadership in ways that make it more broad and also
more specific. Some conceptions of leadership, such as those calling for
visionary, inspiring or transformational leaders are too abstract and
misleading. *What's Worth Fighting For in Leadership for Change?* provides a
more specific analysis of leadership that broadens the concept and sets
out corresponding guidelines for action that will enable many leaders to
flourish in order to create effective schools for the future.

# What's Worth Fighting For In Your School?

Michael Fullan
Andy Hargreaves

Teachers College, Columbia University
New York and London

Published in the United States of America by Teachers College Press, 1234 Amsterdam Avenue, New York, NY 10027

Originally published in Canada by the Ontario Public School Teachers' Federation, 1260 Bay St., Toronto, Ontario, M5R 2B7.

ISBN 0-8077-3554-X

Printed on acid-free paper

Manufactured in the United States of America

03 02 01 00 99 98        8 7 6 5 4 3

# CONTENTS

# FOREWORD

Recently a teacher friend of mine asked me if there was a book written with the teacher's perspective in mind—one that would be useful in helping her school to change itself into a learning and a caring community that worked together for the benefit of all its students. I remember saying that *What's Worth Fighting For in Your School?* is the only book I know that gets at the important issues with which a school faculty must contend in a way that excites teachers to talk about and work on those issues and to invent how, why, and in what manner they will engage in their own process of school improvement.

Students of educational change quickly learn that while there is no list that will tell you precisely how to change a school, there is a set of issues with which all faculties must contend. And they are all contained in this one small monograph: How can teachers build an authentic collaborative culture? How can "collegiality" as opposed to "congeniality" become the operating norm in school? How can teachers become leaders? In what ways can an assessment of one's school program and environment become the starting point for change? How can professional development be intrinsic to the work of improving the school and not an extrinsic set of workshops unrelated to the life of the school? And perhaps most importantly, how can teachers work for improvement and still have time for their personal lives?

As thousands of others have, use this book to begin the struggle for a school culture that's "worth fighting for."

—Ann Lieberman

# PREFACE TO THE SECOND EDITION

This is the first in a trilogy of books designed to help teachers and principals "fight for" fundamentally positive changes that will benefit themselves and their students.

Paradoxically, while there are major forces in society "pushing for change," few educators are better off—even those who are genuinely interested in reform. If anything overload, isolation, fragmentation of effort, and increasing despair describe the lot of most teachers. The mounting forces for change include:

- A focus on *new outcomes* defined less in terms of traditional content and more in terms of teaching for understanding and performance in a changing world
- Movements toward *self-managing* schools and a self-regulating teaching profession with less dependence on outside bureaucracy
- As school system regulation is declining, there is more talk about reinventing teacher *professionalism* with increased standards of practice along with more collaboration and continuous professional learning
- Massive expansion in *information technology* accompanied by greater global access to ideas and people
- *Multicultural and gender politics,* which bring new styles of leadership and more visibility to issues of equity.
- Rapid, complex, multilinear changes in the *workforces* that make occupational choices out of reach to some and land mines to others.

Teaching is both a caring and an intellectual profession. But many caring teachers turn into "moral martyrs," cheerless workaholics, or disillusioned cynics as they encounter relentless, debilitating odds. And while knowledge is becoming more sophisticated and potentially more powerful, teachers still do not experience their teacher preparation or ongoing working conditions as intellectually inspiring or problem-solving enterprises.

We believe that the education profession is at a turning point, and that quantum changes in the nature of the profession as a profession are for the first time both essential and possible. But these changes are not inevitable. Our premise is that teachers and principals themselves must ultimately make them happen. No one else can be relied on to get it right. This does not absolve others from responsibility. Indeed, we have some critical messages for system administrators, politicians, community members, and others. But our bottom-line belief is that by placing the initial onus for action on teachers and principals, greater and more effective pressure to act can be brought to bear on the system as a whole.

What are the basic changes in the teaching profession that are needed? They involve new mind sets, knowledge-bases, and day-to-day dispositions and actions that should characterize the profession of the future. This is what we map out in our trilogy of books. We start with *What's Worth Fighting For in Your School?* Schools are not now learning organizations. By and large they are not interesting and fulfilling places to be either for teachers or for students. Teachers and principals can change this. This monograph lays out some of the core starting points and most powerful levers for change. We want to get at some basic underlying issues. We want to be comprehensive. And we want to be clear and practical. We want to promote understanding, insights, and action. Required solutions will be both collective and individual in nature. Paradoxically, there is neither enough collegiality nor enough individuality in the growth of teachers. As we shall see, collegiality and individuality are not incompatible. They can and must go together if we are to improve our schools. Our message is about working together for improvement. It is that individuals and groups of teachers and principals, with or without help, must, in Bruce Joyce's phrase, "crack the walls of privatism" among themselves, while at the same time working on and respecting their own and others' individual development.

Our study starts in Chapter 1 with an examination of the problem; this serves to set the stage for probing more deeply into issues and solutions. The second chapter, entitled "Total Teachers," enables us to understand teachers in more holistic terms than we often do, both as individuals at any point in time, and as people experiencing a 35- or 40-year career. The third chapter, "Total Schools," examines the social and working conditions of teachers and principals. We pursue the seeming paradox of individuality and collegiality, showing the strengths and weaknesses of each. Ultimately, we argue that they must be reconciled in ways that draw on what each has to offer for improving schools.

The final chapter focuses on what to do to improve things. Drawing on discussion in the previous sections, these "Guidelines for Action" are divided into three sets—for teachers, for principals, and for other educators who work outside the school. The challenge for schools, teachers, and their leaders, as we approach a new century, is the challenge of developing what we call *interactive professionalism* in our schools. Within interactive professionalism:

- Teachers as a group are allowed greater powers of discretion in making decisions with and on behalf of the children they know best.
- Teachers make these decisions with their colleagues in collaborative cultures of help and support.
- Joint teacher decisions extend beyond sharing of resources, ideas, and other immediate practicalities to critical reflection on the purpose and value of what teachers teach and how.
- Teachers are committed to norms of continuous improvement in their school.
- Teachers are more fundamentally accountable as they open their classroom doors and engage in dialogue, action and assessment of their work with other adults inside and outside their schools.

The challenge of interactive professionalism is the challenge of continuous school improvement. It is a process that leads in turn to gains in student achievement. No one working in and with our schools should evade this challenge: It is a challenge that involves us all, one on which we can all take positive action, even in the most apparently unsympathetic and unsupportive environments.

The second book in the trilogy is *What's Worth Fighting For "Out There"?*, beyond our schools. School boundaries have already become much more porous and permeable. One day they may dissolve altogether. Professions—and teaching is no exception—have no tradition of working in open, proactive, collaborative ways with the wider community, where those with whom they work are seen as part of the solution not part of the problem. Professions are often insular and self-serving. They are not used to being held accountable to anyone but themselves. Though they may yearn for it, they do not seem to know how to build a wider sense of purpose and commitment.

While our first book says that schools have failed to capitalize on the strengths of people, to forge collaborative relationships, and to build real senses of community among them, *What's Worth Fighting For "Out*

*There"?* shows why we need to broaden the commitment to collaboration and community beyond the walls of the school itself. The book clearly indicates that in a world of growing complexity and rapid change, if we are to bring about significant improvements in teaching and learning *within* our schools, we must forge strong, open, and interactive connections with communities *beyond* them.

We describe the possibilities and practicalities of working more effectively with parents, employers, universities, the world of technology, and the wider profession. But not all so-called partnerships are productive or powerful. Many are cynical, superficial, opportunistic, or exploitative. Positive educational partnerships, we believe, are morally centered, emotionally engaged, and well thought out. Going *wider* beyond the school in ways that work well for teaching and learning therefore also involves going *deeper* into the heart of our practice. It means rediscovering and recognizing the passion that makes good teaching, revisiting and reviewing the moral purposes that guide that teaching, and reflecting with others on how we can improve teaching together. It means all of us, in our schools, our school systems, and our communities, rethinking and recommitting to teaching as a moral, passionate, and reflective profession. The closing "Guidelines for Action" in *What's Worth Fighting For "Out There"?* show just what it means to go wider *and* deeper in this way.

The final part of our trilogy is *What's Worth Fighting For in Leadership for Change?* Using the previous two books as a foundation, we redefine leadership in ways that make it both broader and also more specific. Some conceptions of leadership, such as those calling for visionary, inspiring, or transformational leaders, seem to us to be wrong. They equate leadership with leaders—qualities with individuals—and create images of leaders as superheroes whom few of us could ever emulate. Other conceptions of leadership, like instructional leadership or stewardship leadership, seem to be on the right track but are impractically abstract. We provide a more specific and grounded analysis of leadership for the future, one that includes all educators, not just an administrative elite, and we set out corresponding guidelines for action that will enable many leaders to flourish in good schools of the future.

The writing style in the *What's Worth Fighting For?* trilogy is not abstruse or academic, but is steeped in what we think are boundary-pushing ideas of research and practice. We do not offer simple steps or easy recipes, but the ideas are accessible, making teachers realize that they are in a profession that is emotionally passionate, deeply moral, and intellectually demanding.

Educational reform has failed time and time again. We believe that this is because reform has either ignored teachers or oversimplified what teaching is about. And teachers themselves have not yet taken the initiative to build the new conditions necessary for reversing a trend that has overburdened schools with problems, and ironically added insult to injury by overloading them with fragmented, unworkable solutions. Teachers have been too busy responding to the latest forays to steer a bold and imaginative course of their own.

This is a time in the evolution of schools and teaching when the future of the teaching profession is "up for grabs." Most people have come to the realization that an improved status quo will not do the job. It is a time for teachers as impassioned moral change agents to fight for the positive preconditions that will shape the profession for the next era: an era in which the learning of teachers will become inextricably bound to the learning of those they teach.

# Chapter 1

# The Problem

**There is simply not enough opportunity and not enough encouragement for teachers to work together, learn from each other, and improve their expertise as a community.**

## Teacher 1

My wife and I were talking about the fact that we have collectively 45 years of teaching experience and nobody — this time excepted — has ever asked us our opinion about anything, where it could actually be put into action. And yet I've got to have more experience with junior [children] than a lot of the people who are telling what I should be doing with them. And I think that is very frustrating ... I think I could help and I could bring a lot to it and nobody ever asks, no one ever asks what we think. They just go ahead and proclaim and we have to follow. I think that part of it is really frustrating. There's a lot of dissatisfaction in teaching.

## Teacher 2

A second teacher reflected on a recent experience of being involved in the cooperative planning of a whole-school focus on "Olympics":

That was very involved. We ran a special sports day outside, and we went to the arena ... and we had a Calgary day at school, and we had pancakes. We had it written up in the paper and everything. It was really quite a job. We certainly learned a lot about planning ourselves, and I think we felt pretty proud, because some schools did nothing or very little, and we were very involved with it. Of course, I'm biased, but I think the school atmosphere here benefits from the kind of family atmosphere we have ... We do things together. There's a lot of junior/primary/senior togetherness in that respect and I don't see such clearcut rivalries between seniors and juniors, and juniors and primaries ... I think it's because of staff unity and the way the principal sees the school as a unit, not as separate little divisions.

1

These are quotations from two teachers, two Canadian teachers, interviewed by one of us in a recent study of how elementary teachers use their preparation time, and how much they work with their colleagues in that time (Hargreaves and Wignall, 1989). The first quote comes from a teacher who complained of not being involved in decisions that affected his work; of not having his expertise recognized; and of being dumped on by an uncaring administration. The second teacher was a teacher who was involved with and felt valued by her colleagues; a teacher with confidence, but not over-confidence in her own skills and abilities; and a teacher who felt respected as a professional in the school community.

One system. Two teachers. Two schools. As different as night and day. These differences are important. They have implications for the ethics of how teachers, as professionals, should be treated. They raise questions about how schools should be led and who should be involved in that leadership. Perhaps most important of all, though, the differences have implications for the very quality, effectiveness and excellence of teaching in our schools—for how teachers relate to and engage students in the daily process of learning. As we shall show, involving teachers in their schools, supporting and valuing what they do, and helping them to work more closely together as colleagues are not just worthwhile humanitarian things to do for their own sake. They also have an impact on the quality of teaching and learning in our classrooms.

The focus on teacher development, the creation of curriculum leadership roles, the development of peer coaching schemes, the introduction of mentor programs, experiments with collaborative planning, and the growth of school-based management and decision making all provide testimony to the ways in which many schools and school systems are seeking to involve teachers more in the life and work of the school outside the classroom, to have them take more responsibility for the policies and practices that are created there.

At the same time, there has been greater imposition of national and provincial curriculum priorities, and appraisal and test schemes to monitor and assess both teachers and students. This simultaneous bottom-up and top-down tension in bringing about reform is a symptom of fundamental dilemmas and problems in bringing about educational change. We see six basic problems in this struggle:

1. Overload
2. Isolation
3. "Groupthink"
4. Untapped Competence (and the neglect of incompetence)
5. Narrowness in the teacher's role (and the problem of leadership)

6. Poor Solutions and Failed Reform

## 1. The Problem of Overload

Teachers are keenly aware that their job has changed immensely in the last decade or so. Teaching is not what it was. Expectations have intensified. Obligations have become more diffuse. In the study on how elementary teachers use their preparation time, teachers spoke extensively about this issue.

Here is how one teacher described some of the important ways that teaching had changed for her over the years.

Teaching is changing so much. There's so much more social worker involved in your job now than there ever was before. So many problems, behavioural and social problems, that are sitting in your classroom that have to be dealt with before you can ever attempt to start teaching. I don't think a lot of people realize that... it's really a changing job... and I don't think a lot of people who've never been in a school and seen a school run know exactly what a person puts up with in a day.

The effects of special education legislation and the mainstreaming of special education students into regular classes caused particular concern.

I find my workload now is much heavier than it used to be. I just think that although there are times that I know I need to stop, I can't. I have to get things done... I think that part of it is the changing expectations of teachers. Large class sizes—I have 29—and when you figure that goes from a Special Ed kid, to enrichment, to ESL, it's a lot of kids that you always seem to be on the tear.

The changing composition of teachers' classes over the years, has had implications not only for discipline and stress but also for the complexity of programming and preparation.

You're always being told that you're constantly responsible for the children. You need to know where they are and what they're doing. You have to be able to program for all the different abilities in your classroom.

Add to this the diverse and ever-changing ethnic composition of classrooms, unstable home and community conditions for children from all social classes, and poverty and hunger, and the classroom becomes a microcosm of society's problems. Accountability to parents and administrators has increased these senses of pressure among teachers.

Especially at this school, we have parents who are very demanding as to what kind of program their children are getting, how it's being delivered, how the test was marked that you sent home...So I find that you have to be very accountable to them as well as to the kids and to the administration too...It takes a lot of thinking through ahead of time ...as to how you're going to mark a paper or present something.

Teachers and principals are dangerously overloaded. More "social work" responsibilities, greater accountability and having to deal with a wider range of abilities and behaviours in their classrooms are now all part of the teacher's lot. Also, because of the knowledge explosion, and because of what we now expect teachers to cover in the curriculum, the values and style of the one classroom-one teacher tradition are no longer relevant for the modern elementary school teacher. Even if they ever did, elementary teachers can no longer reasonably be expected to cover all areas of the curriculum by themselves. To have expertise in math and in language, in science and in music, in art and in computers and in drug and sex education, for example, is too much to expect of even the most skilled and flexible teacher.

Giving elementary and particularly primary students access to other specialists during their own teacher's preparation time has been seen as one way to deal with this particular problem. But as many of the teachers interviewed in the prep time project themselves said, there are limits to how many specialists young primary students can meet without damage being done to the continuous, caring relationship they have with their own teacher.

Advisorship, consultancy and curriculum leadership at the school level are beginning to emerge as alternative solutions to the expertise problem. Here, elementary teachers, with support from outside the school, take responsibility for developing particular curriculum areas with their colleagues, advising their colleagues on resources and approaches, and for working alongside them to implement new initiatives.

Finally, and ironically, innovations-as-solutions exacerbate the overload problem. As if adding insult to injury, fragmented solutions, faddism and other bandwagon shifts, massive multi-faceted, unwieldly reform, all drive the teacher downward. The solution becomes the problem. Innovations are not making the teacher's job more manageable. They are making it worse. Overload of expectations and fragmented solutions remain the number one problem.

As teachers face up to rising and widening expectations in their work and to the increasing overload of innovations and reforms, it is important that they work and plan more with their colleagues, sharing and developing their expertise together, instead of trying to cope with the demands alone. In this emerging conception of the teacher's role, leadership and consultancy are part of the job for all teachers, not just a privilege allocated to and exercised by a few. This conception has gained strength at the level of theoretical discussion but it remains underdeveloped in practice. In the meantime, the problem of overload worsens.

## 2. The Problem of Isolation

Teaching has long been called "a lonely profession", always in pejorative terms. The professional isolation of teachers limits access to new ideas and better solutions, drives stress inward to fester and accumulate, fails to recognize and praise success, and permits incompetence to exist and persist to the detriment of students, colleagues and the teachers themselves. Isolation allows, even if it does not always produce, conservatism and resistance to innovation in teaching (Lortie, 1975).

Isolation and privatism have many causes. Often they can seem a kind of personality weakness revealed in competitiveness, defensiveness about criticism, and a tendency to hog resources. But people are creatures of circumstance, and when isolation is widespread, we have to ask what it is about our schools that creates so much of it.

Partly, privatism is a matter of habit. It is historically ingrained in our working routines. In the preparation time study, many teachers we spoke to could not imagine and had never really thought of any working arrangement other than teaching alone (Hargreaves and Wignall, 1989). The alternatives had never been experienced. Sometimes, physical isolation is unavoidable because of the buildings. Portables in particular can isolate teachers from their colleagues, making them overly protective and possessive about their own classes. As one of the prep time study teachers put it:

> Part of it, being in portables is, you never have team teaching. Even the fact that...this is what I find is the isolation...if I have to go to the washroom, I can't even leave my portable...You get very mothering...because they're your family and you have this little house...Nobody comes. Nobody goes. So you become your own little body of people.

This physical isolation is also revealed in the segregated classroom of so many of our schools—what Lortie (1975) called the traditional "egg-crate structure of schooling". Classrooms tend to isolate teachers. This is no accident. As educational historians have pointed out, the nineteenth century "batch-system of production", where isolated teachers taught fixed programs to age-segregated groups of children, was designed

5

as a way of disciplining and controlling the masses. This outdated tradition of isolation has unfortunately come to be regarded as the "normal" way to teach in many schools. The habit is hard to break.

It is harder to break still when teachers are overloaded and feel pressured. Here's how one of the teachers in the preperation time study put it:

> *Teacher:* It's funny, though, you get at your classroom and into your grade level and you don't realize what's going on in some of the others because you're kind of absorbed in you own stuff. Sounds kind of selfish, doesn't it?
>
> *Interviewer:* Why?
>
> *Teacher:* I think it's just because there's so much to do and you get to the point of—'well, that doesn't concern me'—and there's so much to do in my own class that I spend all my time thinking about that.

The problem of isolation is a deep-seated one. Architecture often supports it. The timetable reinforces it. Overload sustains it. History legitimates it. Later, we will review evidence that links the widespread presence of isolation and privatism to safer, less risk-taking methods of teaching and to poorer standards of student achievement. We therefore believe that cracking the walls of privatism is one of the basic issues worth fighting for. There is simply not enough opportunity and not enough encouragement for teachers to work together, learn from each other, and improve their expertise as a community.

### 3. The Problem of "Groupthink"

In response to the problem of isolation, greater collegiality is becoming one of the premier improvement strategies of the 1990s. There is plenty of evidence to show that collegiality and collaboration among teachers is indeed part and parcel of sustained improvement. Little (1981), for instance, has convincingly described how school improvement is achieved when:

> Teachers engage in frequent, continuous and increasingly concrete and precise *talk* about teaching practice (as distinct from teacher characteristics and failings, the social lives of teachers, the foibles and failures of students and their families, and the unfortunate demands of society on the school). By such talk, teachers build up a shared language adequate to the complexity of teaching, capable of distinguishing one practice and its virtue from another...
>
> Teachers and administrators frequently *observe* each other teaching, and provide each other with useful (if potentially frighten-

ing) evaluations of their teaching. Only such observation and feedback can provide shared *referents* for the shared language of teaching, and both demand and provide the precision and concreteness which makes the talk about teaching useful.

Teachers and administrators *plan, design, research, evaluate and prepare teaching materials together*. The most prescient observations remain academic ("just theory") without the machinery to act on them. By joint work on materials, teachers and administrators share the considerable burden of development required by long-term improvement, confirm their emerging understanding of their approach, and make rising standards for their work attainable by them and by their students (Little, 1981, 12-13).

We continue to find two things. Collegial schools are powerful forces for change, yet they are also in the minority (Joyce & Showers, 1988, Rosenholtz, 1989). We will explain these strong forms of collaboration in Chapter 3.

Yet paradoxes prevail and, as collegiality gets increasingly advocated, we begin to see its downside. Despite demonstrable benefits, collegiality is not without its problems, a number of which are quite fundamental. There is nothing *automatically* good about collegiality. People can collaborate to do good things or bad things or to do nothing at all. People can find themselves collaborating for the sake of collaboration. *"Contrived collegiality"*, as we shall call it later, can gratuitously take teachers away from valuable activities with students. And, contrary to popular opinion, it can *reduce* innovation and imaginative solutions to individual situations, as susceptibility to the latest chosen innovation and "groupthink" carry the day. As basic psychology tells us, groups are more vulnerable to faddism than are individuals.

The pressure of the group — whether for tradition or innovation — is clearly portrayed in Doris Lessing's (1986) *Prisons We Choose to Live Inside:*

People who have experienced a lot of groups, who perhaps have observed their own behaviour, may agree that the hardest thing in the world is to stand out against one's group, a group of one's peers. Many agree that among one's most shameful memories are of saying that black is white because other people are saying it (p. 51).

The unthinking self-suppression of one's own intuition and experiential knowledge is one of the major reasons why bandwagons and ill-conceived innovations flourish (and then inevitably fade, giving change a bad name). It is for this reason that we see the individual as an undervalued source of reform. Lessing puts it this way: "it is my belief that it is always the individual, in the long run, who will set the tone, provide the real development in society" (p. 71).

Collegiality then, can sometimes be less an opportunity than a constraint. Instead of evolving as a valued way of working, it is sometimes imposed as an inflexible system. Working alone has its valuable moments. It is often underrated. We should not throw it out altogether. Indeed the capacity to think and work independently (as well as collectively) is essential to reform. The psychologist Anthony Storr (1988) makes this case well in his analysis of the power and necessity of *solitude*. Interpersonal relationships, he argues, do not constitute the only path toward personal fulfillment. The capacity to be alone is a sign of great emotional maturity, "linked with self-discovery and self-realization; with becoming aware of our deepest needs, feelings and impulses" (p. 21). Teacher change and teacher development, we will argue, is very much bound up with the development of the total person. Interaction is a crucial stimulus here, *but only a stimulus, not the solution.*

Storr also shows how solitude can be a source of personal meaning and creativity. New personal meaning is at the heart of successful innovation, especially under circumstances of frequent change:

> The capacity to be alone is a valuable resource when changes of mental attitude are required. After major alterations in circumstances, fundamental reappraisal of the significance and meaning of existence may be needed. In a culture in which interpersonal relationships are generally considered to provide the answer to every form of distress, it is sometimes difficult to persuade well-meaning helpers that solitude can be as therapeutic as emotional support (Storr, 1988:29).

And,

> Learning, thinking, innovation, and maintaining contact with one's own inner world are all facilitated by solitude (p. 28).

As one engages in interactive professionalism it is essential that development and change are grounded in some inner reflection and processing. Otherwise we can too easily become alienated from our own deepest needs and feelings (Storr, 1988:28).

Consistent with this analysis of solitude as a source of creativity and change, is one of the ten megatrends of the 1990s identified by Naisbitt & Aberdene (1990), "the triumph of the individual" who "changes him or herself first before attempting to change society". Naisbitt & Aberdene make this powerful observation: "Individuals today can leverage change far more effectively than most institutions" (p. 298).

We don't want to overstate this case for personal change before social change. Individuals don't have limitless powers to change things, whatever the circumstances. Throwing yourself repeatedly against impregnable walls of bureaucratic resistance and indifference will only lead to burnout. We are not advocating futile heroics, only personal courage. Such courage requires calculated risk in conditions that offer *some* opportunity for change. Individuals often underestimate their power to change things.

We believe many of these conditions for improvement are now in place. We see all over the world in the 1990s that individuals, spontaneously connecting with other individuals, and creating new groups and alliances, are a far more potent force for revolutionary change than formal institutions. This includes those institutions that claim to be pursuing reform. The same will be true of educational reform.

There is a growing sense of the need for fundamental change in teaching, in curriculum, and in educational leadership, at all levels in the educational system. Existing structures and traditions are becoming destabilised as the primacy of academic subjects becomes questioned, as management becomes less centralised, and as patterns of leadership undergo change. Increasingly, opportunities are wide open for individual teachers to realize their power through other individuals within and across their schools.

Solitude, personal development, and individual creativity are critical. Sorting out one's own individual stance toward improvement is just as important as deciding on collective responses. Individual disagreement and difference should sometimes be sponsored, rather than repressed, by the group. The value of fresh insight and expertise and of some individual diversity, is not always reflected in our promotion practices, which tend to reward the loyal and faithful of our own system against contenders from elsewhere. Our schools need the growth and learning that comes from individual diversity and creativity from within and outside our own school boards. We must experiment and discover better ways of working together that mobilize the power of the group while at the same time enhances individual development. We must use collegiality not to level people down, but to bring together strength and creativity.

So we must fight for collegiality, but not naively. We must protect and promote the individual too.

## Appraisal schemes that implicate 100% of the staff in order to detect a small percentage of incompetents are a gross waste of time.

**4.    The Problem of Untapped Competence (and Neglected Incompetence).**

Isolation means two things. Whatever great things individual teachers do or could do go unnoticed, and whatever bad things they do go uncorrected. Many of the solutions to teaching problems are "out there" somewhere, but they are inaccessible. We can't see them. We recently heard an observation attributed to an African: "Everytime an old person dies, a library burns". Veteran teachers are grossly under utilized. Cynicism retires, but so does wisdom. New teachers with their combination of idealism, energy and fear are also underutilized, as the conservative tendencies of survival take their toll, and already begin to shape their careers towards the lower limits of what could be possible. Any solutions will have to tap into and propel what teachers at all stages of their careers have to offer. This unseen pool of existing expertise is one of the great untapped reservoirs of talent—it can fuel our improvement efforts, and it is right under our noses.

However, if you open up classrooms to find excellence, you also risk exposing bad practice and incompetence. While this risk is real, the actual scale of the incompetence problem is much smaller than the fears to which it gives rise. How many teachers do you think are irretrievably incompetent? It is likely no higher than 2% or 3%. Many teachers are very effective. Their problem is lack of access to other teachers. Access would mean that they could become even better while sharing their expertise. Many other teachers are competent but could improve considerably if they were in a more collaborative environment. If such an environment existed from the very beginning of their careers they would be dramatically better. Those teachers who are ineffective have either become so through years of unproductive and alienating experiences, or were ill-suited for teaching from the beginning. Imposing punitive appraisal schemes for all is like using a sledgehammer to crack a nut. It reduces "appraisal" to the lowest common denominator. Appraisal schemes that implicate 100% of the staff in order to detect a small percentage of incompetents are a gross waste of time. Ironically, the anxiety they generate can also hold back the excellence of the many as they become reluctant to take risks for fear of punishment.

Interactive professionalism exposes problems of incompetence more naturally and gracefully. It makes individuals reassess their situation as a continuing commitment. Separate schemes for dealing with the seriously incompetent are in any case available. Any appraisal schemes should be decidedly focused on growth and development. Anything else wins the odd battle, but loses all the wars. We can't act like teachers don't know what they are doing, without this becoming a guaranteed self-fulfilling prophecy. Even appraisal schemes couched in terms of growth can generate an atmosphere of conservatism if they are perceived to have negative undertones.

In sum, it is important to utilize our existing expertise and learn from each other more effectively. The message is to fight for access to each other's ideas, to assume that people will improve under these conditions, and not to tolerate those very few who, in the final analysis, fail to respond.

## 5. The Problem of Narrowness in the Teachers' Role (and the Problem of Leadership)

Traditionally teaching has been a "flat" career. The only way to expand one's role was to move away from the classroom into administration. There are two fundamental problems in this tradition. First, spending many years in one's classroom without substantial outside stimulation reduces commitment, motivation and effectiveness. Good ideas and innovations developed by individual teachers are often inaccessible to others in the profession. Spending year in and year out performing the same role is inherently deadening. Twenty years of experience doing the same thing is only one year of experience twenty times over.

Second, for classrooms to be effective, schools must be effective. Teachers are a big part of the school. As individuals and groups of individuals, they must therefore take responsibility for improving the whole school, or it will not improve. If they don't, their individual classrooms will not improve either, because forces outside the classroom heavily influence the quality of classroom life: forces like access to ideas and resources, organizational and timetabling arrangements, and sense of purpose and direction. Barth (1990:131) states it this way:

To assert one's leadership as a teacher, often against forces of administrative resistance, takes commitment to an educational ideal. It also requires the energy to combat one's own inertia caused by habit and overwork. And it requires a certain kind of courage to step outside of the small prescribed circle of traditional "teacher tasks," to

11

declare through our actions that we care about and take responsibility for more than the minimum, more than what goes on within the four walls of our classrooms.

Related to this second issue is the problem of the gap between leaders and led. When responsibility is left solely to formal leaders, it overloads them, resulting in incorrect and frequently imposed solutions. Such a system also fails to prepare younger teachers for future leadership roles.

At a time of mounting expectations, heightened accountability and accelerating change, educational leaders have no one with whom to share the burden of responsibility. In *What's Worth Fighting For in the Principalship?* we described how this overload was the key problem of the modern principalship, creating dependency and helplessness among many of those who occupied the role. Staging the teacher career more gradually and giving teachers earlier experience of leadership, increases the opportunities for delegation and reduces overload, enabling principals to be more selective and to set clearer priorities for what they do.

Preparation for leadership is also related to gaps in responsibility. In the unstaged elementary school, transition from classroom teacher to vice-principal is often too sharp, too sudden. A more valuable and effective system of preparation for principalship would, and now increasingly does involve giving regular teachers much more experience of leadership, administration and policy development earlier in their careers, when they are still very much rooted in their classroom roles.

The answer to these problems is new forms of teacher leadership based on interactive professionalism and a view of teacher education as a continuum or career-long process. Current examples of the proliferation of leadership roles for teachers include:

1. Induction programs that support and extend innovative behaviour of new teachers.
2. Mentor roles for experienced teachers that result in just as much growth for the mentors as for those with whom they work.
3. Coaching projects and work norms that value working together, offering help, and discussing difficulties even among mature and experienced staff, and restructuring efforts in which staff and principals together attempt to reorganize the school to support continuous improvement.

Unfortunately, as we will discuss later, the solution can sometimes become the problem. New roles can be superficial, contrived, overly bureaucratic. Deeper change involves broadening the conception of the teacher so that individual teachers bring even more resources to bear on the classroom as a result of being routinely connected to a larger web of professional deliberations. Teacher leadership, defined as the capacity and commitment to contribute beyond one's own classroom, should be valued and practised from the beginning to the end of every teacher's career. There are few more basic things to fight for.

> **However noble, sophisticated, or enlightened proposals for change and improvement might be, they come to nothing if teachers don't adopt them in their own classrooms and if they don't translate them into effective classroom practice.**

### 6. The Problem of Poor Solutions and Failed Reform

Most attempts at educational reform fail. Neither bottom-up nor top-down strategies seem to work. There are many reasons for this failure:

- The problems themselves are complex, and not easily amenable to solutions given the resources at hand.
- Time lines are unrealistic because policy-makers want immediate results.
- There are tendencies toward faddism and quick-fix solutions.
- Structural solutions (eg. redefining the curriculum, increasing assessment and testing) are often preferred, but they do not get at underlying issues of instruction and teacher development.
- Follow through support systems for implementing policy initiatives are not provided.
- Many strategies not only fail to motivate teachers to implement improvements but also alienate them further from participating in reform.

In short, the conditions for mobilizing teachers as a resource for reform simply do not exist. Many of us in the business of school improvement and educational change have painfully come to realize what should have been obvious over the years—that the heavy burden of responsibility for change and improvement in schools ultimately rests on the shoulders of the teachers. However noble, sophisticated, or enlightened proposals for change and improvement might be, they come to nothing if teachers don't adopt them in their own classrooms and if they don't translate them into effective classroom practice.

Knocking down walls, as many Ontario elementary schools did in the wake of the Hall-Dennis report in the 1970s, is not enough to bring about change. Nor is writing supposedly teacher-proof curriculum packages, as many new math and science programs did in the 1960s and 1970s. Teachers can always shut the door and get on with what they want to do anyway. Educational change that does not involve and is not supported by the teacher usually ends up as change for the worse, or as no real change at all. In the end, it is the teacher in his or her classroom who has to interpret and bring about improvement. Where change is concerned, the teacher is clearly the key. Leadership that neither understands nor involves the teacher is therefore likely to be leadership that fails. Excluding teachers from the task of leadership or the process of change is in this sense neither practical nor politic. As Sarason (1990:5-7) argues in his account of *The Predictable Failure of Educational Reform*:

> Schools will remain intractable to desired reform as long as we avoid confronting...their existing power relationships...Altering power relationships requires a degree of insight, vision and courage that is in short supply among leaders of complicated organizations ...Ignore those relationships, leave unexamined their rationale, and the existing "system" will defeat efforts at reform.

Yet, the precise way we should do this is not at all clear. Widespread participation in decision-making often results in aimlessness, confusion, frustration and burnout—a sense that we are not getting anywhere and that valuable time is being taken away from the classroom. We believe that the entire proposition must be rethought. Focussing on the total person and the total school as we do in this monograph is one way of ensuring that solutions are not piecemeal or misplaced.

## Conclusion

"The problem" is therefore not one problem but many. It is a problem of promotion-blocked teachers in mid-to late-career, who are losing energy and enthusiasm, as well as motivation and morale as classroom challenges gradually fade into repetitive routines. It is a problem of new teachers struggling to survive alone in their classrooms, regressing to safety and mediocrity as they try to ward off possibly adverse judgements from their colleagues. It is a problem of narrowly "inservicing" teachers in particular skills without taking into account the total teacher in terms of age, gender and personal values. It is a problem of teaching being a changing job, of having wider and more diverse expectations which requires more consultation and contact between teachers, their colleagues and a range of other adults—contacts for which they often have insuffi-

14

cient training, time and support. And it is a problem of leadership—of finding more gradual, developmental ways to train and prepare teachers for bringing about improvements, and of transforming the role of the principal from that of a meeting-bound bureaucrat, to an instructional leader who can work closely with his or her staff in developing and implementing common educational goals.

A common theme runs throughout the issues raised in this chapter. This is the overwhelming need for greater involvement of teachers in educational reform outside as well as inside their own classrooms, in curriculum development and in the improvement of their schools. In the rest of the monograph, we will develop a vision of what this kind of involvement might look like. We will see that involvement itself is not enough. It is the *kind* of involvement, the particular way that teachers work together as a community that really matters, if meaningful improvement in our schools is to take place.

# Chapter 2

# Total Teachers

---

## Total teachers are not perfect teachers.

In recent years, most of us have started to acknowledge the teacher's importance in bringing about change. We have paid more attention to staff development, to the growth of teachers. But mostly, we have done this in a limited and even misguided way. Indeed, many of our approaches to staff development are part of the change problem more than they are a solution to it. Many staff development strategies have been just as fragmented, non-involving and as oblivious to the real needs and concerns of teachers, as the other innovation strategies they were meant to supplement or supplant (Fullan, 1990, 1991, Little, 1990).

A high proportion of staff development efforts are specific, focused on particular innovations and isolated from each other. They tend to be offered in a set of self-contained, cafeteria-like options to target groups of schools and teachers. Because staff development officers are often relatively low in the pecking order of supervisory officers, packaged programs, specific initiatives and one-shot workshops can be attractive and practical because they do not impinge awkwardly on curriculum matters, or on the continuing organization of the school. No one else's territorial rights are infringed. As a result, training in techniques of effective instruction is tackled separately from the development of mentor systems, which is in turn tackled separately from peer coaching. And this is tackled separately again from leadership training.

Such strategies of staff development isolate initiatives from each other and from the wider, institutional context into which they are inserted. In an uncongenial work context which has unsupportive working relationships and is suspicious of innovation, specific staff development initiatives are almost certainly doomed to failure. More careful integration of staff development strategies with strategies of school improvement is now needed—integration which takes account of the whole school as a complex and changing institution.

Many staff development initiatives take the form of something that is done *to* teachers rather than *with* them, still less *by* them. When new initiatives like cooperative group work, active learning, or destreaming are undertaken, principals and administrators often speak of "inservicing" their teachers, as if they were lowly residents in some kind of educational farmyard. Such top-down approaches to staff development embody a passive view of the teacher, who is empty, deficient, lacking in skills, needing to be filled up and fixed up with new techniques and strategies.

Approaches of this kind seriously underestimate what teachers already think, know and can do. They underestimate the active way that teachers relate to their work. They ignore the way that teachers' approaches to their work are deeply grounded in the accumulated learning of experience, in the meaning that their work and the way they approach it has for them as people. They do not recognize the important moral and social purposes they want to fulfil through their teaching.

Staff development is often driven not by strategies likely to improve the all-round quality and performance of schools, but by administrative and political pressures to get preferred, sometimes "faddish" innovations implemented quickly (Pink, 1989). The adverse effects of this top-down process of staff development therefore raise important questions not just about the sensitivity of staff developers themselves but also about who controls innovation. Top-down mandates may preclude what it is that teachers are able to develop, in that they often concentrate the responsibility for curriculum development in the school board office.

## Many staff development initiatives take the form of something that is done to teachers rather than with them, still less by them.

Because much staff development is fragmentary in nature, rushed in its implementation, and top-down in its imposition, it addresses only a fragment of the teacher. It ignores different needs among teachers related to years of experience, gender and stage of career and life. It treats the teacher as a *partial* teacher, not a *total* teacher. It fails to grasp fully how teachers grow and how teachers change. In the patterns of staff development we have described, a lot of effort has been invested in improving teachers' technical skills, through peer coaching initiatives, and classroom management programs, for instance. But in the eagerness to bring about change and improvement, four other important aspects of the total teacher have been overlooked, so that teaching and change have been misunderstood. These are:

1. The teacher's *purpose*
2. The teacher as a *person*
3. The real world *context* in which teachers work
4. The *culture* of teaching; the working relationships that teachers have with their colleagues

We treat the first three aspects in this chapter. The fourth component—the culture of teaching—has much to do with the total school and is the subject of chapter 3. We caution the reader that the ideas in chapters 2 and 3 must be taken into account together. It would be misleading to derive strategies from any one set of ideas in isolation from the others.

## 1. The Teacher's Purpose

Teaching is not just a collection of technical skills, a package of procedures, a bunch of things you can learn. While skills and techniques are important, there is much more to teaching than this. The complex nature of teaching is too often reduced to matters of skill and technique, to things that can be packaged, put on courses, easily learned. Teaching is not just a technical business. It is a moral one too. There are two senses in which this is true.

First, teachers are among the most important influences on the life and development of many young children. They play a key role in creating the generations of the future. With the decline of the church, the break-up of traditional communities, and the diminishing contact that many children have with parents who can "be there" for their children on a regular basis, the moral role and importance of today's teacher is probably greater than it has been for a long time.

There is also a second sense in which teaching is deeply moral, irreducible to efficient techniques and learned behaviour. This has to do with the nature of teachers' decisions and judgements. In teaching, as in a number of other occupations, the core of its professionalism is best defined and described not in terms of pay or status or qualifications but in terms of the distinctive kinds of action and judgements that professionals typically make. As Schon (1987) puts it, professional action involves *making discretionary judgements in situations of unavoidable uncertainty*.

Teachers, like urban planners or architects or psychotherapists, are continuously involved in making innumerable, practical, everyday small decisions which are of great importance to their clients and their colleagues. For these decisions, there are few or no clear rules of thumb that can be clearly listed in a manual, and applied in a systematic way from one situation to the next. To confront a student or avoid the confrontation. To let the child's discovery run further or to intervene and direct it. Decisions about discipline, classroom management, classroom fairness, the freedom of the child versus the need for teacher intervention and support, all embody complex social, philosophical, psychological and moral judgements. Yet they are also judgements that have to be made and passed second by second, in the complex hurly-burly of the classroom. It is the application of accumulated skill, wisdom and expertise in the specific and variable circumstances of the classroom which defines much of the teacher's professionalism — the teacher's capacity to make informed discretionary judgements in the rapidly shifting environment of the classroom.

Embracing this view of teaching and teachers' work suggests approaches to leadership, administration and professional development which respect, support and build upon teachers' capacity to make informed discretionary judgements in the classroom with the students they know best. By contrast, approaches which seek to regiment and regulate the teachers' actions; to constrain and contract their opportunities for discretionary judgement and to standardize the process and the products of learning, undermine teachers' professionalism and the moral principles on which it is based.

Because teaching is a moral craft, it has purpose for those who do it. There are things that teachers value, that they want to achieve through their teaching. There are also things they disvalue, things they fear will not work or will actually do harm to the children in their charge. Teachers' purposes motivate what teachers do. Sadly, reformers and change agents often overlook teachers' purposes. They do not give teachers' purposes a voice. They treat those purposes as if they are unimportant or don't exist.

Change involves values and purposes associated with what is being changed. Will it be helpful or harmful? Is it realistic or impractical? These are important matters for teachers and their voices deserve a hearing. When no such hearing is granted or encouraged, teachers understandably become frustrated and dispirited. One teacher in the preparation time study, described his experience of being "inserviced" where "We were just hearing philosophy. I wasn't hearing any practicality. And I like to see practicality and philosophy go together, so I'd like to try some of the ideas out, so if I have questions, I can ask them about it; and I'm not getting that...." In another case, "there was a lot of questions, but they were just ramming everything down your throat."

Ignoring or riding roughshod over teachers' purposes can produce resistance and resentment. Yet when teachers display these kinds of reactions, and have reasonable questions about what they are being asked to change, these reactions are too often regarded as problems of technical competence, fear of change itself, or diffidence about working with others. Problems with the change come to be seen as problems with the teacher. Problems of fundamental *will* are interpreted as problems of mere technical *skill*.

We are not saying that the teacher's sense of purpose is sacrosanct. Indeed, for many teachers their sense of purpose is vague, misplaced, neglected or poorly developed. Teachers rarely confront and attempt to clarify and develop their sense of purpose either individually or collectively. Under the isolated conditions of teaching, many can lose sight of their sense of purpose, or otherwise fail to develop it.

The key question then is how best to appreciate, confront and develop a clearer, stronger sense of purpose in teaching. Herein lies another dilemma. On the one hand, we want teachers to question their own existing practices, and be open to new ideas and potentially better ways of doing things. On the other hand, we need to respect and build on the knowledge and ideas that teachers already have, or we run the risk of bypassing existing valuable practices, and alienating teachers as we do so. We can use Joyce and Shower's (1988) well-known staff development model to illustrate both sides of the problem. Joyce and Showers advocate a model of theory-demonstration-practice-feedback-and coaching or follow through. They focus on models of teaching which have "known potential for increasing student learning", including cooperative learning, mnemonics, concept formation etc. In a recent project, Joyce and Showers have been working in a school-district to help bring about school-wide classroom and organizational improvements. They have made considerable progress in introducing new practices to teachers. In so doing, they report the substantial presence of anxiety among teachers and explain it like this:

> We now believe that anxiety is a natural syndrome that arises from two sources; first, fears of exposure and incompetence in the more public teaching environment and, second, the giving up of reasons why learning cannot be improved (Joyce et al., 1989: 23).

Fair enough. For some teachers anxiety is attributable to these factors. And teachers need to consider new ways of teaching that promise to be more effective than what they might currently be doing. But teachers are also exposed to scores of instructional innovations through the normal course of staff development and inservice, all of which claim to "have sound bases". So, in addition to straightforward anxiety about fear of exposure, many teachers have quite sensible doubts and disagreements about the validity of what it is they are being asked to do, how it fits into what they are doing, and how it relates to the array of models that they see coming and going. Are the new skills practical and desirable? Will they work in my classroom? How do they relate to other alternatives? What matters here is *not just whether the particular model is valid or not, but how it connects to a teacher's overall sense of purpose in the particular situation in which he or she is working.*

We worry about approaches to improvement whose main task is to implement one or more models of instruction without treating teachers initial beliefs about teaching and learning as equally important. The problem of externally developed innovations has two implications. First, since the system is overloaded with alternatives, administrators and teachers alike are vulnerable to ad hoc solutions, and "expert" advice. The first implication is that practitioners must become better critical consumers of external innovations, not because promoters of innovation are always suspect (although some are), but because the variety of choices must be related to and *integrated* with their own sense of purpose and context. They should also be wary of researchers and developers who make claims of exaggerated "certainty" for their knowledge base (Robertson, 1991). Second, sponsors and developers of particular models should use procedures to learn from and build on the practical wisdom of teachers. One example which integrates research and practitioner knowledge in this way is Richardson and Anders' (1990) staff development project "to introduce research-based understandings of reading comprehension into teachers' thinking and practices". In their approach, teachers are encouraged to examine their own empirical and value premises of what they have been doing in comparison with premises extracted from research. Here, examination of the research knowledge modifies teachers' practice, and examination of teachers' practical knowledge raises important critical questions about the research. Learning does not move in one direction only, from research to teaching. It is a respectful, two-way process.

Instructional innovation is not the only way that teachers' purposes can get overridden or misunderstood. Policy makers and administrators are also often poor at understanding what motivates teachers, what kind of purposes drive them in their work. Greater opportunities for promotion (through schemes such as career ladders), and the introduction of merit pay for excellent classroom teachers, for instance, have been two innovations which have been widely proposed in the United States and, in some cases, implemented as ways of motivating classroom teachers. Yet, these innovations are based on false presumptions of what motivates many classroom teachers, especially in the elementary years. Promotion appeals only to some and can only be offered to a few. Merit pay appeals to the pursuit of personal gain — not a high priority for many elementary teachers beyond a certain minimum level. Neither of these innovations really come to grips with what are the main motivators for most teachers: the quality of the work and the working environment itself.

The greatest satisfactions of elementary school teaching are found not in pay, prestige or promotion but in what Lortie (1975) called the *psychic rewards* of teaching. By this, he meant the joys and satisfactions of caring for and working with young people. The teachers in the preparation time study talked a lot about the pleasures of being "with the kids". They spoke of the immense pleasure of hearing a child read his or her first word or sentence. One teacher commented that when children cheered on being given a new project, "that was its own reward". Several were eager to say that while they had been critical of certain ways in which preparation time was allocated or used, they did not want the interviewer to think they disliked teaching. Teaching gave them immense satisfaction, they said. For some, it was "a wonderful job." Even when bureaucratic pressures and constraints seemed overbearing, it was the kids and being with the kids that kept these teachers going. A number questioned the value of meetings, mandatory cooperative planning and other administrative initiatives insofar as these took them away from their kids.

These psychic rewards of teaching are important. They are central to sustaining teachers' sense of value and worth in their work. In many ways, what the primacy of these rewards points to is the centrality among elementary teachers of what Gilligan (1982) calls an *ethic of care,* where actions are motivated by concerns for care and nurturing of others and connectedness to others. The ethic of care is extremely common, but not exclusive to women, says Gilligan. Women, of course, make up the vast proportion of elementary school teachers. It is, in many respects, the commitment to the ethic of care which brings many teachers to elementary teaching in the first place. What are its implications for administratively-driven change?

For one thing, administrative justification to collaborate with colleagues often appears to be presented less in terms of an ethic of care, than in terms of a contrary *ethic of responsibility*. Professional obligations are prominent. Improvements to planning and instruction are stressed. Effectiveness is emphasized. It may be that where elementary teachers are fearful that commitment to collaborative planning, for instance, might prejudice their capacity to care for their own class of children, perhaps more attention should be paid to ensuring that such planning demonstrably *supports* teachers in their caring and teaching role. More than this, it may be important administratively and in the school community to make care, as well as responsibility, one of the central principles that underpins collaboration amongst colleagues. Elementary teachers should be persuaded by word and by deed that there are other kinds of caring to give and receive in the school community in addition to caring for children.

The ethic of care has even more interesting implications for a second administrative issue, which is the provision of scheduled preparation time for elementary teachers within the school day. In recent years, Ontario teacher federation representatives have pressed hard for continuing increases in teacher preparation time in elementary schools. The prep time study showed universal teacher approval of the benefits already won. But when asked whether prep time should be extended still further, a number of teachers were at least ambivalent about the impact that additional preparation time might have on the coherence of their children's program, the stability of the classroom atmosphere and the quality of instruction. They were genuinely torn in their commitments and their desires. They could certainly do with more time, they said. But they also worried about the negative consequences that extra time away from class would have for instruction and classroom "flow," as they called it. As one teacher put it:

I guess having taught when there wasn't any, I'm so grateful for having some. I think it's hard — I could say "Yes, I could use more." But you've got to remember that the more time you're out of the classroom — they get different teachers. And there are three teachers right now in my class. Is this too much for the kids? Is it too much for the classroom teacher trying to keep track of all these other people? I wonder if I had much time away if I would feel I was losing something with the kids. And yet I could certainly use the time.

Such responses do not constitute a case for putting an end to more preparation time extensions. But they do raise questions about whether such additions need to entail more time away from class. Virtually all teachers we interviewed seemed to assume this would be the case. Proposals to extend preparation time, therefore, seemed to place their concerns with care, their psychic rewards at risk. We have to watch very carefully that our most well-intentioned commitments to effectiveness and improvement don't undermine what many teachers value most here — the time and opportunity to care for and teach their children.

What we are saying is that we must open up the possibilities for teachers to examine their own purposes and practices in comparison with those of others (and of research) in a way that enhances rather than subtracts from the caring and psychic rewards of teachers in their own classroom. Joint work with other teachers in preparation time that focuses on, and stays close to children is one valuable way out of this dilemma.

Administrative change in education, we believe, should therefore pay much more attention to the teacher's purpose. It should:

- give voice to the teacher's purpose.
- actively listen to, indeed sponsor, the teacher's voice.
- establish opportunities for teachers to confront the assumptions and beliefs underlying their practices.
- show preparedness to listen and learn from what teachers have to say about change.
- avoid creating a culture of dependency among teachers by overrating the expertise of published research and underrating the practical knowledge of teachers.
- avoid faddism in the form of blanket implementation of new instructional strategies whose worth and appropriateness are administratively treated as being above criticism.
- empower teachers and their schools to regain substantial decision-making responsibility for curriculum (the key domain of purpose and value), as well as for instruction.
- create a community of teachers who discuss and develop their purposes together, over time, so as to develop a common sense of mission in their schools.

We are not suggesting we move from a state where teachers' purposes are disregarded, to one where they are uncritically endorsed and celebrated. Researchers, administrators and teachers themselves, none of these groups has a monopoly on wisdom. But the wisdom of teachers is often considerably undervalued compared to the wisdom of the other two groups. Much more can be done to allow and actively encourage critical dialogue between these groups in the change process. This may well slow down the pace of change, but it will likely create changes that are more effective, that teachers are more committed to, and that last.

**Total teachers, we propose, are most likely to emerge, develop and prosper in total schools, in schools which value, develop and support the**

## judgement and expertise of all their teachers in the common quest for improvement.

### 2. The Teacher as a Person

Teachers, we have said, are more than mere bundles of knowledge, skill and technique. There is more to developing as a teacher than learning new skills and behaviours. As teachers sometimes say to their students, they are not wheeled out of a cupboard at 8:30 in the morning and wheeled back in at 4:00. Teachers are people, too. You cannot understand the teacher or teaching without understanding the person the teacher is (Goodson, 1991). And you cannot change the teacher in fundamental ways, without changing the person the teacher is, either. This means that meaningful or lasting change will almost inevitably be slow. Human growth is not like rhubarb. It can be nurtured and encouraged but it cannot be forced. Teachers become the teachers they are not just out of habit. Teaching is bound up with their lives, their biographies, with the kinds of people they have become.

Many factors are important in the making of a teacher. Among them are the times in which teachers grew up and entered the profession, and the value systems and dominant educational beliefs that went with those times (compare the 60s to the 80s here, for instance). Also important is the stage in life and career that teachers are at, and the effect this has on their confidence in their own teaching, their sense of realism, and their attitudes to change. The teacher's sex is another factor, in particular the way that teaching and work in general for men and women are often bound up with very different sorts of lives and interests.

This view of the teacher as a person has crucial implications for our understandings of change, professional development, and working relationships between teachers and their colleagues. We want to focus on two of these implications: the ways we often misjudge the competence, commitment, and capacity of our colleagues; and the excessive and unrealistic expectations we sometimes have of our colleagues concerning their involvement in schools and their commitment to change.

First, in teaching, as in life, we are quickest to judge those who fail rather than those who succeed. When teachers are new to the job, incompetence can be excused or at least tolerated. They are, after all, only learning. Experienced teachers who should have matured with their years in the classroom, get away less lightly. Where incompetence is persistent rather than temporary, it is rarely excusable. Almost every reader of this monograph will have known at least one teacher in mid to late career, whose competence and commitment have been in doubt among their colleagues. We have a glossary of graphic labels for such teachers — "dead wood", "burned out", "time-servers", and "past-it"! Such labels do not really explain these teachers' difficulties, though. They explain them *away*. They are not labels that invite action, that suggest solutions. They are labels that legitimize inaction, that signal abandonment of hope. The fault is presumed to be in the teacher, deeply ingrained in their personality. Little point, therefore, in trying to change them. Not much you can do about bad teachers, especially bad *old* teachers, except wait for them to leave, retire or die! "If only I could get some new teachers ...." or "wait until my new teachers arrive ..." — these are principals' stock responses to this apparently irremediable problem.

Yet have you ever wondered what these 55-year old "time servers" were like when they were 35, or 25? Were they just ticking over then too? Were they that cynical? Is it possible that they were once as bright-eyed and idealistic as many of their younger colleagues are now. And if they were, what happened to them in the meantime? Why did they change? Have you ever wondered what it might be like to be one of these people, ever wondered about the man or the woman behind the mask?

Some of the reasons for the transformation, of course, have to do with aging. Sikes' (1985) analysis of the aging process within the "life-cycle of the teacher" is instructive. One of the age-phases she describes is between 40 and 50 or 55:

> It is during this phase that it becomes apparent whether or not the work of establishing occupational career, family and identity begun in the twenties and thirties has been successful; and it tends to involve self re-appraisal, questioning what one has made of one's life... (Sikes, 1985:52)

This is when disappointment can set in. It is also a time, particularly towards the later years, of sheer decline in physical powers which puts morale and enthusiasm very much to the test. As one of Sikes' teachers expressed it: "The kids are always the same age and you gradually get older and older... And unfortunately too, their capacity for life, their energy remains the same as yours diminishes..."

Disillusion and disappointment tend to go with the aging process in the teacher's unfolding career. But there is nothing natural or inevitable about this. Much depends on the particular experiences these teachers have had, on how their schools have treated them. To some extent, aging is a cultural process of learning, of interpreting the ways that other people repeatedly treat you. The disillusioned are partly products of their own mortality, but they are also products of their schools' management — responsible as such management is for the quality of experiences and treatment these teachers receive over the years. Trees do not kill themselves. "Dead wood", rather, is usually the product of an infertile, undernourished environment. In this sense, schools often end up with the staffs they deserve.

Huberman (1988, 1991) has produced some research findings which speak revealingly to the particular issue of career cycles of teachers. Huberman interviewed 160 secondary school teachers in Switzerland, about the ways in which their careers impacted on their attitudes to innovation and instruction. He found that most teachers in mid-to-late career were unlikely to embrace innovation with enthusiasm, and unlikely to make any radical changes in their approaches to instruction either. Some, the "defensive focusers" and the "disenchanted" as Huberman calls them, were deeply cynical about change. They had (accurately) predicted the demise of past innovations, had stayed well clear of them then and continued to do so now. Or they had invested a lot in them only to be "sold out" and "let down" as the innovations collapsed and the innovators themselves moved on to further and higher glories.

Other teachers — Huberman called them "positive focusers" — were not so dismissive, but were nonetheless tempered in their reactions and enthusiasms. At this stage of their career, current innovations were not the first they had encountered. They had seen several innovations come and go. Experience gave them good reason for caution. At their age and stage of career, they were also feeling distinctly mortal. The men were learning at this late point what many women had understood earlier. They recognized the importance of establishing a balance between the personal and professional life, of leaving time to tend the garden, smell the roses. These "positive focusers" did not oppose or ignore innovation. But they did respond to it cautiously and selectively. They would not put their "all" into it. They would not abandon instructional practices in which they had grown confident and competent over decades. But they *would* use insights that came from small scale experiments with their practice, and they were open to working with selected colleagues on targetted improvements in their own classrooms. Under the right conditions they would make improvements to what they did. As Huberman observes, most strategies for staff development do not tap into and build on this source of innovation.

Age, stage of career, life experiences, and gender factors make up the total person. They affect people's interest in and reaction to innovation and their motivation to seek improvement. When we introduce new teaching methods, we often ignore these differences and treat teachers as if they were a homogeneous lot. In the process, we often devalue large segments of the teaching population. This problem is especially important at a time when many new teachers are entering the profession, new teachers on whom many an eager principal is staking his or her hopes for future improvement. Principals have been waiting a long time for this infusion of new blood into the system. It is clear that a serious and unexpected danger looms ahead also—the danger of ostracising and alienating existing staffs of more mature teachers who may not embrace with as much eagerness and energy as their junior colleagues the new methods and approaches favoured by their principals and their boards. These teachers deserve both our understanding and respect in a system which should be cautious about granting inflated importance to very particular approaches to instruction like cooperative learning or "whole language" at the expense of all others which have preceded them. Without such understanding it is likely that many teachers will disengage from their work, will ignore or resist change, and will help create divided schools of "old" and "new" teachers, polarized into opposing factions.

At the other end of the spectrum, the failure to recognize the special needs and contributions of beginning teachers can also have a disastrous, lasting impact on their motivation and confidence to become good teachers and good colleagues. Mentors are not just there to support their proteges but also to learn from them. Teaching is inherently difficult. Even the most experienced need help. From their recent training, their university subject knowledge and their willingness to try things out under the right conditions, new teachers will have much to give to experienced teachers. We must also be careful not to take advantage of new teachers and their seemingly endless energy by loading them with extracurricular responsibilities and giving them the worst classes. This is a sure path to early burnout.

A second sense in which reform often glosses over the personal lives, interests and backgrounds of teachers, concerns the expectations we have for change and commitment. Teaching is very important. However, there is more to life than school. Life interests and responsibilities beyond teaching must also be recognized. In our enthusiasm to involve staff more and more in the life of the school, and to commit them to change within it, we should not forget the other legitimate calls on their time and commitments, which in the long run may well make them better people and teachers for it.

There are important gender implications here. We have seen from Huberman's (1988) and Krupp's (1989) work that women's experience has important implications for understanding and questioning how men in school systems often related to their careers. It suggests the personal benefits and advantages for many men that might come with a less narrow concentration on career advancement, and with it, a greater responsibility for the domestic labour and childcare that might help many of their female partners who work in teaching and elsewhere (Acker, 1989). In dealing with gender irregularities in teaching, much of the policy emphasis has been on encouraging more women to apply for promotion, on creating promotion quotas, and so on. These are proper and helpful forms of action. But their focus is very much on making the characteristically male educational career more available to women. What analysis of the experience of women teachers also suggests is that individual development of all teachers, men and women, may also be well served by questioning and revising our norms in schools and school systems of what constitutes proper commitment for a teacher, of how much involvement in the wider affairs of the school life is reasonable and desirable, given various personal circumstances. Commitment to continuous improvement is important. Becoming a professionally omnivorous workaholic is not!

We need to be particularly cautious about models of teacher development which interpret that development in terms of single hierarchies where there are implied progressions from sin at the lowest levels, to grace at the top. Such hierarchies, while appearing to be scientifically neutral, are heavily loaded with value. An example is Leithwood's (1990:75) model of teacher development which describes level 6, the highest level of professional development, as involving teachers "participating in a broad range of educational decisions at all levels."

Some critics might say this is a counsel of perfection for any teacher. But our own criticism is more than merely saying the expectation is unrealistically high. In our view, it also presents a model of "good development" which may be value-laden, and which is unintentionally ageist, sexist and biased against more classroom-focussed teachers who are uninterested in conventional career advancement. Leithwood's model does not allow for the importance of balancing the professional life with the personal one and for the designation "professionally developed" to be attached to teachers who choose this pattern. It is a model which does not allow for many female or older teachers, who forsake heavy involvement in administration and wider school affairs for the satisfaction of classroom commitment, to be regarded as the "most developed" group. It is a model which presumes only one path to excellence where there are, in fact, many.

We will claim later that every teacher must work at improvements outside their own classroom, but this need not always be done on a large scale.

So we should fight for a broadening of expectation, for an acknowledgement that there are several versions of excellence and more than one route to achieving it. We should also temper some of our expectations in the pursuit of excellence, not as an act of defeatism, but as an exercise in realism where we abandon the pursuit of swift, drastic change for change which is more modest in its scope, yet more widespread and enduring in its impact. Put another way, sweeping blanket reforms, running to tight timelines, that are insensitive to the wider aspects of the teacher's life and career and that do not address the teacher as a person, are unlikely to be successful.

## Schools often get the teachers they deserve.

What, in summary form, have we learned from this discussion of the teacher as a person?

- that teaching behaviours are not just technical skills to be mastered, but behaviours that are grounded in the kinds of people teachers are.
- that among the many factors which shape what kind of people and teachers, teachers become, one of the most important is how their schools and their principals treat them.
- that schools often get the teachers they deserve. Teachers who are devalued, discarded and disregarded become bad teachers. Ironically, such an approach also permits the seriously incompetent to be ignored.
- that we need to value and involve our teachers more. There is something to value in almost every teacher. We should identify it, recognize it and reward it.
- that valuing our colleagues involves more than being more caring and sympathetic. It also involves extending what we value. Faddish innovations, narrow views of excellence, rolling bandwagons of whole language or cooperative learning which presume only one good way to teach, divide insiders from outsiders, and create alienation and incompetence among those who are excluded.
- that while not any route to excellence will do, many routes are possible. Salvation has more than one road. This applies to instruction and to professional development alike.

- that extensive involvement in school decision-making does not constitute the highest level of professional development for all teachers. Maintaining a balance between work and life, concentrating on expanding one's own classroom repertoire rather than getting consumed by school-wide innovation, is just as worthy a form of professional development for many teachers.
- that massive commitment to whole-school change is an unrealistic goal for many teachers — for many of those in later career, for instance. Modest but persistent attempts to expand teaching repertoires and to improve practice in association with colleagues may be a more realistic objective.
- that meaningful and lasting change is slow. Changing people is not achieved overnight. It requires patience and humility on the part of administrators.

Acknowledging the teacher's purpose and understanding and valuing the teacher as a person, we want to suggest, should therefore be vital elements underpinning any strategy of staff development and school improvement. It is one of the keys to unlocking motivation and to helping teachers confront what it means to be a teacher.

## The separation of curriculum from instruction is an historical legacy that can become an instructional fallacy. It is time to bring them back together.

### 3. The Context of Teaching

For teachers, change is not a paper plan or an elegant flow chart. It must happen in the busy and complicated worlds of their own classrooms. A consultant or a teacher educator can do a superb lead lesson, but it is the teacher who has to emulate that lesson hour after hour, day after day, week after week. A video on cooperative group work with computers can demonstrate excellence in strategies of instruction, but it is the teacher who must somehow carry out that group activity alongside all the other pressing demands of other students in his or her classroom. Change is too often idealized; thought of in self-contained systems and packaged too neatly. It needs to be dealt with in ways that are much more sensitive to the real world demands of the *context* of teaching.

To understand the teacher's teaching, it is important to understand these circumstances, to understand the *context* in which the teacher works. We need to know how the teacher's environment influences the teacher's teaching. We need an *ecological* understanding of teaching—of how teaching develops to suit the environment, and in what ways we can and should change that environment if we want to change what goes on there.

Three aspects of the context of teaching are particularly important. *First,* some aspects of the context of teaching vary. Teaching is not always the same. Different approaches to instruction or classroom management are appropriate in different settings —as many intermediate teachers asked to take over a Grade 1 or 2 teacher's class during preparation time have discovered to their surprise (Hargreaves, forthcoming). Many teachers in this situation discovered that the classroom management strategies they had always found perfectly effective with young adolescents were not at all effective with Grade 1s & 2s. For the first time in many years, some of these teachers experienced discipline problems! Their existing teaching repertoire would not do. They had to learn new management strategies for their new circumstances. This reminds us that teaching strategies cannot be standardized. Sensitivity to context is vital when attempting to improve instruction.

Failure to come to terms with the varying contexts of teaching can lead to simplistic, idealistic approaches to improvement —and then to disappointment and disillusion when they fail. The belief that because some schools are successful at making particular improvements, and therefore any school can be just as successful is a false and dangerous one. For instance, the existence of exemplary models of staff collegiality in some schools should not be interpreted as meaning that norms of collegiality can be established just as easily in other schools. Reviews of existing research in this field, in fact, suggest that collegiality tends to prosper in middle class environments where resources are better, working environments more congenial, staff more carefully selected, and a sense of hope and possibility more strong. This is not an argument for abandoning attempts to create more collegial environments in less favoured schools. But it is a case for the realistic acknowledgement that the challenge of collegiality in working-class schools is likely to be different and probably greater than in those exemplary instances of good practice that are held up as beacons for the rest of us to follow.

A *second* important aspect of the context of teaching is its realism and practicality. Most teachers are interested in classroom excellence, in challenging their students, in making learning active and fun. Total teachers are not perfect teachers. Teachers are also interested in maintaining their health and managing their stress. They are interested in not wearing themselves out, and in giving themselves breathing space to recover by assigning seatwork or other routine activities, for instance. Most teachers recognize the importance of actively engaging students in their learning, but they also see the need to settle those same students down with quieter, steadier work, if they have become over-excited by the lesson or activity before.

While these points seem obvious, principals and other administrators may fail to see them on given occasions. Dropping in unannounced on a teacher's lesson, it is easy for the principal to take a dim view of the teacher found dictating notes or administering a spelling test, or assigning handwriting drills. But this is a view taken out of context, which judges the teacher against ideal models of instruction rather than against the ongoing practicalities of the context with which the teacher is dealing. These may include the teacher's health or energy level, his or her need to catch up with marking or other administrative work, or to deal with the spillover effects of the previous drama lesson, or to recover from a confrontation with a troublesome student. These and other factors not immediately visible may be responsible for those seemingly poor practices. Of course, where virtually all of a teacher's teaching is characterized by poor practice, administrators have good cause to be concerned. But we should not judge teaching without first understanding the context which gives rise to its use.

A *third* aspect of the context of teaching is the same for virtually all teachers. These contextual characteristics set important boundaries around what teachers can do, around the realistic possibilities for innovation. Many of these realities, such as classroom isolation, are strongly institutionalized. They have deep historical roots. But while they look like "givens" they need not be fixed. Indeed, as Sarason (1982) advises, questioning the apparent "givens" of school is one of the most important activities we can undertake as a prelude to change. Things can be otherwise. Let's look at some of these apparent "givens" that influence what teachers do. We will pick out just a few. *Class size* is one obvious factor, but contrary to popular belief, marginal, yet still costly reductions in class size of 2-3 students do not lead to decisive gains in student achievement. Only when numbers of around 15 students or fewer are attained do real improvements occur. Such reductions are just not viable economically. But working with smaller groups can be achieved through using cooperative learning methods, creative arrangements for team teaching, teachers covering colleague's classes, and the like.

*Time* is another important resource which can bolster or block innovation. Small increments in time for teachers to work together outside

33

class within the school day can make a real difference to improvement efforts (Fullan, 1991). Time to plan with colleagues, to observe someone else's teaching, and to work with individual students or smaller groups can all help improve the quality of instruction. Increases in scheduled preparation time have certainly helped these activities to develop, although prep time does not itself guarantee that they will (Hargreaves, forthcoming). Principals and vice-principals can also help release teacher time for other activities by covering teachers' classes occasionally. By doing that, they also show their commitment to the activity for which the teachers are being released.

Another factor which can place boundaries around the possibilities for improvement is the *curriculum*. One of the distinctions we most take for granted in education is that between curriculum and instruction. In doing this, we lay an administrative basis for dividing them up into different domains of responsibility. School board administrators and consultants become responsible for devising and developing the curriculum. Teachers are assigned the responsibility for instruction, for the business of delivering it.

In Ontario, administrative control of the curriculum stretches back to the foundation of public school systems in Upper Canada when substantial powers for curriculum determination were invested in school board officials ( Fullan, Connelly & Watson, 1990). This tradition, where the teacher's chief responsibility is for instruction, not curriculum, has become deeply entrenched. We believe there are good reasons for questioning it. Our main reason is that prescribed curriculum guidelines developed at board level or above tend to foster dependency among teachers. Closely-prescribed, content-laden guidelines, tend to lead teachers to concentrate on *coverage*, on "getting through" the material (Hargreaves and Earl, 1990). An emphasis on "coverage" in turn often leads to teaching methods which run fewer risks of not getting to the facts.

Preoccupation with coverage can have undesirable effects on the quality of instruction. In a study of 12 junior-high schools in the U.S., Tye (1985) found that teachers were highly preoccupied with curriculum coverage, particularly in science and social studies.

> The preoccupation with coverage dominated the social studies in our schools. Focus on concept learning and explanation was only moderately evident. Perhaps this was why such a potentially interesting subject was among the least liked subjects by the junior high students in our sample (Tye, 1985:141)

In another recent American study, Ashton and Webb (1986) showed that teachers with a lower sense of "efficacy", a depressed sense of their capacity to have positive effects on their lower-attaining students, were more preoccupied with "covering" prescribed material than were teachers with a higher sense of efficacy. Teachers with a lower sense of efficacy also tended to have lower rates of achievement in basic skills among their students. Feelings of powerlessness which contribute to teachers' lowered sense of efficacy, are often brought about in systems where they have little control over what is taught. Of course, the most creative and dynamic teachers will always find ways of resisting curriculum guidelines and adapting them to suit their own purposes. But the reality for most ordinary teachers is that they do not. For them, detailed guidelines are not frameworks of opportunity but prisons of constraint.

Mandated curriculum guidelines also affect teachers' relations with their colleagues. Getting teachers to work more closely together may be undermined by a curriculum that is seen by teachers as so tightly defined, there is little for them to collaborate about. An administratively controlled curriculum may therefore set important limits to teacher collaboration. Giving more responsibility for curriculum development to teachers and schools may in this respect be one of the most important challenges in changing the context of teaching. The separation of curriculum from instruction is an historical legacy that can become an instructional fallacy. It is time to bring them back together.

To sum up, the context of teaching significantly influences the kinds of teaching you are likely to get and the improvement targets you can reasonably set. Many attempts to improve instruction have been based on psychological theories of learning, which take little account of the social contexts in which learning and teaching have to take place. The price of ignoring the context of teaching in this way is failed idealism in efforts at improvement, guilt and frustration among teachers who cannot meet the standards set for them, criticism of teachers who fail to make the changes expected of them, and erratic leaping from one innovation bandwagon to the next.

The contemporary teaching context is not conducive to mobilizing teachers toward greater and more fundamental efforts at improvement. Sizer (1984:184) gives us an insight into this in his account of *Horace's Compromise*. He portrays an image of a teaching context that is widespread and not at all congenial to improvement:

Teaching often lacks a sense of ownership, a sense among the teachers working together that the school is theirs, and its future and their reputation are indistinguishable. Hired hands own nothing, are told what to do and have little status in their enterprises. Teachers are often treated like hired hands. Not surprisingly they often act like hired hands.

## Conclusion

The critical question, then, is what kind of context is most likely to be supportive of growth and improvement? What kind of context is most likely to acknowledge, respect and build upon the *purposes* of the teacher and the *person* that teacher is, while at the same time making teachers responsive to expectations and new ideas in the wider environment? Different kinds of contexts, leadership and working relationships are needed if continuous improvement is to be secured. The context called for here, we want to suggest, is one that embodies a particular *culture* of teaching, a particular set of working relationships among teachers and their colleagues which bind them together in a supportive, inquiring community, committed to common goals and continuous improvement. *Total teachers,* we propose, are most likely to emerge, develop and prosper in *total schools*, in schools which value, develop and support the judgement and expertise of *all* their teachers in the common quest for improvement. What such a community might look like and how it might be developed are the subjects of the next two chapters.

# Chapter 3

# Total Schools

---

**What is worth fighting for is not to allow our organizations to be negative by default, but to make them positive by design.**

If changing the teacher involves changing the person the teacher is, we need to know how people change. None of us are islands. We do not develop in isolation. We develop through our relationships, especially those with others who are significant for us. These significant others act as a kind of mirror for our developing selves. If our workplaces contain people who matter to us, and are among our significant others, they will have a strong capacity, either positively or negatively, to affect the kinds of people and, therefore, the kinds of teachers that we become.

The key question, therefore, is what kinds of work communities or school cultures[1] are most supportive of teacher growth and school improvement. How do we avoid creating and maintaining negative cultures that inhibit or squelch development and improvement? And how do we establish more positive ones? In this sense, what is worth fighting for is not to allow our organizations to be negative by default, but to make them positive by design.

We will discuss two basic types of school culture — individualistic and collaborative ones - with their very different implications for change and improvement. Then we will take a closer look at collaborative models and discriminate between more and less effective versions of them. We will argue that the teachers' and students' workplace is the key to reform. Schools are not now places where individual and collaborative growth of teachers (and hence of students) can flourish.

---

1. We use the concept "culture" to refer to the guiding beliefs and expectations evident in the way a school operates, particularly in reference to how people relate (or fail to relate) to each other. In simple terms, culture is "the way we do things and relate to each other around here".

# A root cause of individualism has to do with the impossibly high expectations many teachers set for themselves in a job with poorly defined limits.

## 1. The Culture of Individualism

Teaching is not the oldest profession. But it is certainly among the loneliest. As Rudduck (1991) says, "education is among the last vocations where it is still legitimate to work by yourself in a space that is secure against invaders". (p. 31) The most common state for the teacher is not a collegial one. It is a state of professional isolation; of working alone, aside from one's colleagues. This isolation gives teachers a certain degree of protection to exercise their discretionary judgement in the interests of the children they know best. But it also cuts teachers off from clear and meaningful feedback about the worth and effectiveness of what they do.

Isolated teachers may get some feedback from periodic formal evaluations, but these are frequently perfunctory and sporadic. They are not helpful for the ongoing improvement of performance (Hickcox et al.,1988). Their own classrooms and students, therefore, become the main source of feedback for most teachers. But this feedback is notoriously unreliable. Scanning the room for signs of difficulty might supply evidence of one's own effectiveness, but smiles, frowns and droopy eyelids can provide only ambiguous clues at best. Students asking for help can also provide feedback, but it may well be only the bravest ones who will readily confess ignorance to the busy teacher intent on covering the material. And tests, quizzes and exams assess only a limited range of student performance - conveying little about attributes like motivation, enjoyment or enthusiasm.

As it is presently organized, classroom feedback can only mitigate the uncertainties of teaching to a limited extent. A degree of uncertainty is of course endemic to all teaching, which is why it is important to empower teachers with the capacity and flexibility to make discretionary judgements about curriculum, instruction and discipline in their own classes. But uncertainty experienced alone, in enforced isolation, is uncertainty magnified to unhealthy proportions. Moreover, feedback within one classroom has a ceiling effect confined to one teacher's experiences, one teacher's interpretation, and one teacher's motivation to seek improvement.

In her study of 78 elementary schools in Tennessee, Rosenholtz (1989) speaks about "stuck" and "moving" schools. She found that in "stuck" schools, which were not supportive of change and improvement, uncertainty and isolation went hand in hand. Measures of teacher uncertainty, she found, correlated negatively with student learning gains in reading and math over a two-year period (p.128). One of the main causes of uncertainty, Rosenholtz found, was the absence of positive feedback:

> Most teachers and principals become so professionally estranged in their workplace isolation that they neglect each other. They do not often compliment, support, and acknowledge each other's positive efforts. Indeed, strong norms of self-reliance may even evoke adverse reaction to a teacher's successful performance (p.107).

Rosenholtz explains that isolation and uncertainty are associated with what she calls "learning impoverished settings" where teachers are able to learn little from their colleagues, and therefore are not in a strong position to experiment and improve. In these settings, she argues, teachers "held little awareness that their standardized instructional practice was in large part the reason they performed none too well" (p.106). These findings echo those of Lortie, some fifteen years earlier who interviewed 94 elementary and secondary teachers in the greater Boston area and collected questionnaires from almost 6,000 teachers in Dade County, Florida. For Lortie, individualism was pervasive among teachers. Beyond sharing a few practical hints, resources and tricks of the trade, and beyond swapping stories about parents or the kids, teachers rarely discussed each other's work, almost never observed their colleagues teach and did not collectively analyse and reflect on the value, purpose and direction of their work.

Uncertainty, isolation and individualism are a potent combination. Almost by definition, they sustain educational conservatism, since the opportunity and pressure arising from new ideas are inaccessible. Such narrowness of orientation and experience lead to "safe", non-risk-taking forms of teaching that do little to assist student achievement. Where multiple demands are being externally imposed on teachers and their schools, isolated teachers feel powerless in the face of pressures and decisions which they often do not understand and in which they are not involved. This sense of powerlessness eats away at the teacher's sense of his or her own capacity to "make a difference" in children's education. (Ashton and Webb, 1986).

We referred earlier to the need to "crack the walls of privatism" in our schools if we are to bring about successful and lasting change. When teachers are afraid to share their ideas and successes for fear of being perceived as blowing their own horns; when teachers are reluctant to tell others of a new idea on the grounds that others might steal it or take credit for it (or on the assumption that others should go through the same painful discovery process that they did); when teachers, young or old, are afraid to ask for help because they might be perceived as less than competent; when a teacher uses the same approach year after year even though it is not working—all these tendencies shore up the walls of privatism. They limit growth and improvement quite fundamentally, because they limit access to ideas and practices that might offer better ways of doing things. *They institutionalize conservatism.*

Small chinks are appearing in these walls of privatism though. Peer coaching, mentoring, site-based management and other schemes are beginning to bring teachers together. These developments, as we shall see later, are not without their problems, but they are opening up the possibilities.

Beyond these small chinks, however, open collaboration, extensive collegial conversation, mutual observation, and interactive professionalism are not yet an integral part of most teachers' working lives. Only the merest whispers of these things are with us, though even they are better than the silence which preceded them. In the main, as research studies are continuing to show, it is privacy, individualism and isolation that remain the persistent and pervasive conditions of teaching

If we are to tackle individualism, it is important we first understand why it exists. If we do not understand it, we will have little chance of changing it. In our view and in the view of other critics, many of the diagnoses of individualism have been rather simplistic, implying blame on the part of teachers themselves for its existence (Flinders, 1988, Little 1990, McTaggart, 1989). The existence of individualism can too easily be regarded as revealing some kind of flaw in the teacher personality, or as betraying seemingly "natural" qualities of human diffidence and uncertainty. While these things may be true in part, there are also specific features of teachers' work which make individualism perfectly understandable. These work characteristics can be changed, and so, too, can the individualism that accompanies them.

Individual buildings, separated egg-crate classrooms, and isolated portables are all architectural features which can induce individualism and make it hard for teachers to work together. But while open-plan classrooms can make collegiality easier, they by no means guarantee it. Indeed, it is widely known that teachers often go to considerable lengths to reassert their privacy in open-plan environments by closing the screens or stacking up cupboards to make barriers. Two of the root causes of teacher individualism are not at all material though. They are grounded in the traditional norms and conditions of teaching.

The first of these has to do with teachers' experiences of evaluation. Most teachers' first experiences of having other adults in their classrooms are ones of being evaluated while feeling intensely vulnerable in the learning of their craft. However benevolent the supervisor is  in these early days of teaching, it is still a formative period when help gets confused with and sometimes obscured by judgement. In our present positions we work extensively in a professional development capacity with teachers. Frequently we ask teachers to describe and reflect upon formative experiences which they believe have made them the kinds of teacher they are today. A common and striking feature of these teachers' accounts is that of early, unpleasant encounters with evaluation, seen as the infliction of humiliation by those who are supposed to help. (As someone once wryly observed, "the helping hand strikes again"). It is, therefore, not at all surprising that teachers often associate help with evaluation, or collaboration with control. Isolation and individualism are their armour here, their protection against scrutiny and intrusion.

When making moves to establish closer cooperation between teachers and their colleagues, we therefore recommend that help be clearly disassociated from evaluation. This is important, for instance, in the design of professional growth programs. We also advise that teachers and administrators make every effort to build helping relationships that are reciprocal, that do not just run in one direction. In help-giving, it is just as important to receive as it is to give. Like friends who will always do favours for you but never ask for any in return, the help-givers can inflict an unbearable burden of guilt and debt on those who receive the help. If the recipients themselves are never asked for help, the debt can never be repaid. However well intended, help of this patronizing or matronizing sort is help wrapped up with power — a package that ultimately deters those who receive it from ever asking for more.

There are important lessons here for all educational leaders including principals, heads of division, and lead teachers or mentors, for instance. Those lessons are that they should acknowledge and communicate their own needs as help-receivers as well as help-givers, if they are to build effective cooperative relationships with their colleagues. This is often hard for teachers to learn, when their experience in the classroom has been giving help and care not receiving it. Some of the qualities for effective work with adults will be quite different than those for students. Many teachers will have to learn these new qualities in order to be supportive colleagues.

A second root cause of individualism has to do with the impossibly high expectations many teachers set for themselves in a job with poorly defined limits. In recent years, elementary teachers have been faced with a range of mounting pressures and rising expectations for excellence in a widening array of responsibilities. Integrating special education students; working with ethnically and linguistically diverse students; individualizing student programs from the learning disabled to the gifted; coping with growing amounts of "social work" in their role; and dealing with all the preparation and paper-work that has followed in the wake of the accountability movement are some of the pressures that teachers have had to cope with in recent years.

Many of the pressing demands and expectations of teaching also come from within teachers themselves. Many teachers appear to drive themselves in an attempt to meet the virtually unattainable standards of perfection they set themselves. They do not appear to need direction or pressure from above to motivate them in their quest. They drive themselves quite hard enough.

Thus, the teachers' role is being defined by themselves and by others ever more widely, encompassing social and emotional goals as well as academic ones. Goals and expectations defined and understood in such diffuse terms become difficult, indeed impossible to meet with any certainty, yet dedicated elementary teachers strive hard to meet them. As Flinders (1988) puts it:

> More so than other occupations, teaching is an open-ended activity. If time and energy allowed, lesson plans could always be revised and improved, readings could always be reviewed again, more text material could always be covered before the end of the term, students could always be given more individual attention, and homework could always be graded with greater care.

In teaching, patients are never stitched up, bodies never buried, cases never closed.

Working in the service of other human beings and surrounded by diffuse expectations, guilt and frustration become part of the job. As one teacher in the preparation time study remarked:

> Teaching is a profession that when you go home—you always have stuff that you think about. You think "I should be doing this." I feel guilty sitting down half the time.

These unrealistically high expectations, many of them self imposed, seem to us to have two consequences that reinforce individualism. First, teachers do not have time for collaboration. Since there is so much to be done, time to collaborate is taken away from time to meet pressing needs with one's own class. So teachers retreat to the classroom and close the door to meet their obligations—even during break time when they prefer to prepare and work alone rather than plan with colleagues (Flinders, 1988:23)

The second consequence of high expectations and uncertainty is that collaboration becomes risky. If teachers are trapped in pursuit of their own unending aspirations, if they cannot ever do enough in their own eyes, how could they possibly meet the expectations of others? And, if they have given up or resigned themselves to accepting the status quo, they resist intrusion even more strongly. The isolated classroom is a refuge from such collegial judgement, but a refuge that provides little help in addressing the problems of uncertainty.

The flip side of keeping to oneself is the reluctance to give and receive help. Under these circumstances it is hard to have confidence in one's expertise and to be perceived by others as having something to offer. Nowhere is this seen more clearly than when teachers take on some instructional leadership role (resource teacher, curriculum committee, master teacher). McTaggart (1989) interviewed one such teacher:

I don't want to go in with these teachers and say I know how to do this. So I have to be careful what I say. But if someone asks, or if the subject is brought up, I will subtly tell them how I have success in a particular way. I still have to be careful and throw in, "I didn't do this right", or "I could have done this a little bit better". This is part of maintaining a good rapport with teachers (p. 352).

Holding back what you know, being unconfident about what you have to offer, being reticent to seek better ways of doing things and treating teachers like they need help and have little to give are all ways in which the tradition of individualism retards progress, and keeps teaching fundamentally unsatisfying in the long run.

We have said that individualism is not just an attitude of teachers. It is rooted in the very conditions under which the teacher's role has evolved. These traditions are now being challenged. As we turn to new conceptions and strategies of collaboration, our message will be twofold. First, as we seek to eliminate *individualism* (habitual patterns of working alone), we should not eradicate *individuality* (voicing of disagreement, opportunity for solitude, and experiences of personal meaning) with it. Individuality is still the key to personal renewal, which in turn is the foundation for collective renewal. Individuality also generates creative disagreement and risk that is a source of dynamic group learning. Second, we should not underestimate what we are up against in moving toward collaborative cultures. This development represents a fundamental and sophisticated change. It will be easy to get it wrong, and hard to set it right.

For many years, while research on the iniquities of individualism has been in abundance, studies of the benefits of teacher collaboration have been scarce. As individual schools and school boards have started to undertake initiatives in developing collaborative teacher relationships, we are beginning to realize some of the actual benefits, but also some of the obstacles and drawbacks of different kinds of collaboration.

We are first going to examine the power of collaborating because the future of educational reform involves unleashing this greatly under utilized resource. Second, we are going to identify weak and unproductive forms of collaboration because only deep, sensitive, and enduring patterns of teacher collegiality will be worthwhile.

## The Power of Collaboration

Rosenholtz (1989), you will recall, drew attention to two particularly distinctive school cultures in her sample. She called these *stuck* (or "learning impoverished") schools and *moving* (or "learning enriched") schools. To recap, the "stuck" schools were schools with lower levels of student achievement where teachers usually worked alone and rarely asked for help. What of the "moving" schools then?

Rosenholtz showed that in the "moving" schools, teachers worked together more. Most teachers, even the most experienced, believed that teaching was inherently difficult. They believed that teachers never stopped learning to teach. Since most teachers acknowledged that teaching was difficult, almost everyone recognized they sometimes needed help. Giving and receiving help did not therefore imply incompetence. It was part of the common quest for continuous improvement. Having their colleagues show support and communicating more with them about what they did led these teachers to have more confidence, more certainty about what they were trying to achieve and how well they were achieving it.

As Rosenholtz observes, in effective schools, collaboration is linked with norms and with opportunities for continuous improvement and career-long learning: "It is assumed that improvement in teaching is a collective rather than individual enterprise, and that analysis, evaluation, and experimentation in concert with colleagues are conditions under which teachers improve" (p. 73). As a result, teachers are more likely to trust, value, and legitimize sharing expertise, seeking advice, and giving help both inside and outside the school. They are more likely to become better and better teachers on the job: "All of this means that it is far easier to learn to teach, and to learn to teach better, in some schools than in others" (p. 104).

For Rosenholtz, the most important effect of teacher collaboration is its impact on the *uncertainty* of the job, which, when faced alone, can otherwise so undermine a teacher's sense of confidence. Similarly, Ashton and Webb (1986) found that the main benefit of collaboration is that it can reduce teachers' sense of powerlessness and increase their sense of efficacy. Part of Ashton and Webb's study focused on a comparative analysis of a rather traditionally organized junior high school, and a more progressively inclined middle school. Although the two schools catered to students from similar social backgrounds, the middle school secured higher student attainment scores in the basic skills. Ashton and Webb attributed this difference to the teachers' sense of efficacy and their perceptions of their role in the two schools.

In the junior high school, teachers were "somewhat fatalistic" about their students' academic potential. Teachers here saw their pursuit of more ambitious goals earlier in their career as naive. They were more realistic now, they said. Students' failure to comply with academic goals was viewed as a problem of motivation; a problem with the students or their backgrounds.

The middle school teachers had a stronger sense of efficacy: "They were convinced that they could make a significant contribution to the lives of children and were publicly and personally committed to doing so" (p. 106). Middle school teachers had a higher opinion of their profession and its responsibilities. They defined their work more widely - emphasizing personal development as well as academic achievement; work with colleagues as well as work with students. Collaboration among teachers—team teaching and shared decision-making was an organizational feature of this school. Resources and supplies were shared. Planning was done together; scheduled at the beginning and end of the school day. Teachers talked about everything. They thrashed issues out in reaching a common focus. This helped give them a common sense of accomplishment, of belief in their efficacy.

These are not the idiosyncratic findings of two isolated studies. They are confirmed in a wide array of supporting educational research. What is most compelling about this research is how teachers become better teachers in some schools, while teachers in other schools fail to grow or even become worse. This point is clearly made in comparing the attitudes toward teacher learning in Rosenholtz's collaborative or "moving" schools verses those in the isolated or "stuck" schools. In the collaborative schools, "80% of the teachers responded ...that their own learning is cumulative and developmental, and ...that learning to teach is a life-long pursuit" (p. 80). Typical of the comments was "You never stop learning. It's important to learn how to teach something in as many different ways as possible to reach all these students. I'm always on the search for new ideas" (p. 80). Teachers in these collaborative schools sought more ideas from colleagues, professional conferences, and workshops. When troubles arose they were far more likely to seek and receive advice and assistance from other teachers and the principal. Teachers in collaborative schools had greater confidence and commitment to improvement.

By contrast, only 17% of the teachers in isolated schools expressed a sustained view of learning for themselves. They did not act as if there was more to learn, or that they could become more effective teachers by seeking outside ideas.

There is no doubt some selectivity here. Teachers open to new ideas are attracted to "moving" schools. Teachers reluctant to learn may find "stuck" schools safer (but, we venture to say, not more satisfying in the long run). And we will make the point later that it is important to identify and foster openness to learning when selecting future teachers, and when providing their first experiences in initial teacher education programs and first appointments. But the power of the workplace is one arena where the fight for improvement must occur. We know it can be done because there are collaborative schools "out there", albeit in the minority where, "continuous self-renewal is defined, communicated, and experienced as a taken-for-granted fact of everyday life" (Rosenholtz, 1989:74). *Imagine that you would become a better teacher, just by virtue of being on the staff of a particular school—just from that one fact alone* (Little, 1989).

Up to now we have said a number of supportive things about collaborative working relationships and their benefits for schools. But we have not been clear about what collaboration actually looks like for principals and teachers. This is not unusual. Attractive concepts like collegiality and collaboration are often imbued with a global sense of virtue. Vagueness can be helpful at the beginning, as people attempt to sort out the various possibilities. But it can also presage later disillusionment and disappointment if the different hopes and meanings invested in it do not pan out, and the *meaning* and benefits become less clear. It is vital then that we understand the meaning of collaboration.

What passes for collaboration amounts to very different things in different schools. Some of these are likely to reduce teacher uncertainty and increase teacher efficacy. Some of them are less likely to do so. It is important, for instance, that because you have a happy staffroom, because teachers exchange anecdotes about the kids and because teachers provide each other with moral support, you do not presume that you have a collaborative school. The kinds of collaboration that lead to greater effectiveness mean much more than this. Schools where teachers remain isolated and uncertain in their own classrooms are not always overtly unhappy schools in the social sense. Indeed in her account of the "stuck" schools in her sample, Rosenholtz said that the staffrooms in these schools were often happy places. However, the happiness was rooted either in conversations that were broadly social, concerned with non-school activities, or in stories and jokes told about the kids and their parents, often at their expense. There was little professional talk in these staffrooms — no serious discussions of work and its improvement. Clearly, when trying to develop collaborative cultures, contentment should not be mistaken for excellence.

Little (1990) has identified four different kinds of collegial relations among teachers. She describes: (1) scanning and storytelling, (2) help and assistance, and (3) sharing — as relatively weak forms of collegiality. She argues that if collaboration is limited to anecdotes, help giving only when asked, or to pooling of existing ideas without examining and extending them, it can simply confirm the status quo. There is another kind of collegial relation, however.

Little observes that the fourth type—*joint work*—is the strongest form of collaboration (eg. team teaching, planning, observation, action research, sustained peer coaching, and mentoring etc.). Joint work implies and creates stronger interdependence, shared responsibility, collective commitment and improvement, and greater readiness to participate in the difficult business of review and critique. This, says Little, is the kind of collaborative work and culture most likely to lead to significant improvement. In the quest for improvement, other kinds of collaboration may support this basic thrust, but by themselves are likely to be poor substitutes for it.

Little claims that many examples of apparent collegiality represent "weak ties". She cites evidence that coaching and mentoring projects, for example, often are of this relatively superficial, safe and inconsequential variety, and hence have little impact on the culture of the school. We will return to this matter of weak forms of collaboration in the next section, but here we want to emphasize that the search for strong, effective forms of collaboration must create the conditions where teachers can raise and address critical, intrusive questions:

> Bluntly put, do we have in teachers' collaborative work the creative
> development of well-informed choices, or the mutual reinforcement
> of poorly informed habit? Does teachers' time together advance the

47

understanding and imagination they bring to their work, or do teachers merely confirm one another in present practice? (Little, 1990:22).

One of the most insightful accounts of what collaborative cultures look like in practice, has been provided by Nias and a team of researchers in England (Nias, Southworth & Yeomans, 1989). Nias and her team undertook intensive case studies of five primary schools already noted for their positive staff relationships. They taught and observed in these schools for a year. The rich descriptions they built up at these schools provide fascinating, detailed and realistic accounts of what high functioning collaborative cultures look like in practice. Three of the schools comprised fully-functioning collaborative cultures. The five schools were small (up to 12 fulltime teachers) so we must be careful not to generalize. But the configuration of characteristics is instructive of what we are facing in working toward collaborative work cultures. What were these school key characteristics?

What characterizes cultures of collaboration, according to Nias and her team, are not formal organization, meetings or bureaucratic procedures. Nor are cultures of collaboration mounted for specific projects and events. Rather, they consist of pervasive qualities, attitudes, and behaviours that run through staff relationships on a moment-by-moment, day-by-day basis. Help, support, trust and openness are at the heart of these relationships. Beneath that, there is a commitment to valuing people as individuals and valuing the groups to which people belong.

Collaborative cultures are to be found everywhere in the life of the school: in the gestures, jokes and glances that signal sympathy and understanding; in hard work and personal interest shown in corridors or outside classroom doors; in birthdays, treat days and other little ceremonial celebrations; in the acceptance and intermixture of personal lives with professional ones; in overt praise, recognition and gratitude; and in sharing and discussion of ideas and resources.

In collaborative cultures, failure and uncertainty are not protected and defended, but shared and discussed with a view to gaining help and support. Teachers do not waste time and energy covering their backs here. Collaborative cultures require broad agreement on educational values, but they also tolerate disagreement and to some extent actively encourage it within these limits. Schools characterized by collaborative cultures are also places of hard work, of strong and common commitment, dedication, of collective responsibility, and of a special sense of pride in the institution.

Collaborative cultures acknowledge and give voice to the teacher's *purpose*. Ironically, disagreement is stronger and more frequent in schools with collaborative cultures than it is elsewhere, as purposes, values and their relationship to practice are discussed. But this disagreement is made possible by the bedrock of fundamental security on which staff relationships rest — security that allows openness in discussion and temporary disagreement, in the knowledge that continuing relationships will not be threatened by it. In collaborative cultures, the examination of values and purposes is not a one time event, as when staff participate in writing a Mission Statement, but a continuous process that pervades the whole school. Yet disagreement is also made possible by the broad agreements on fundamental values and directions which staff develop and move towards over time. Purposes in collaborative cultures are not entirely idiosyncratic, but gain much of their strength from being developed with and shared by other colleagues.

Collaborative cultures also respect, celebrate and make allowances for the teacher as a *person*. In collaborative cultures, as Nias and her colleagues say, teaching is a personal affair, but not a private one. Staff here willingly reveal some of the more personal sides of themselves. Leaders are also encouraged to do so. Vulnerabilities are voiced; allowances made for personal circumstances, illness, bereavements and bad days. In collaborative cultures of the kind described by Nias et al. the person is not consumed by the group, but fulfilled through it. Purpose and person — those elements essential to teacher competence — are both openly declared and positively developed in the culture of collaboration.

Collaborative cultures create and sustain more satisfying and productive work environments. By empowering teachers and reducing the uncertainties of the job that must otherwise be faced in isolation, collaborative cultures also raise student achievement. Collaborative cultures facilitate commitment to change and improvement. They also create communities of teachers who no longer have the dependent relationships to externally imposed change that isolation and uncertainty tend to encourage. Dealing with change is no longer a choice between uncritical, enthusiastic acceptance or unconsidered rejection. In collaborative cultures, teachers develop the collective confidence to respond to change critically, selecting and adapting those elements that will aid improvement in their own work context, and rejecting those that will not.

What is most revealing in Nias et al.'s findings is the particular configuration of beliefs and behaviours in the highly collaborative schools. *Within these schools the individual and the group are inherently and simultaneously valued.* Individuals are valued, and so is interdependence.

In valuing *individuals* as people, teachers, including newcomers, were made to feel welcome. Teachers showed an interest in each other's personal lives, while respecting the right to privacy. The total person counted.

Allowances were made at work for domestic circumstances such as a husband's or son's redundancy. Staff were tolerant of each other's taciturnity, irritability or unaccustomed inefficiency, they were quick to anticipate the help which might be needed because of, for example, a fit of depression, a painful back, a broken car or a sleepless night. When someone was having a bad day, the appropriate response was to be sympathetic rather than offended. In the collaborative schools there was a pervasive atmosphere of consideration for others. (p. 55)

Individuals were also valued as contributors to others. As one teacher put it:

Working in a team doesn't mean that everybody's the same and everybody's so busy saying yes, yes, yes to one another that nothing happens. That deadens it. You've got to have different personalities and different ideas to spark other people off, but it can be done without aggression (p. 57).

*Interdependence* was valued in two ways: first, in the sense of belonging to a group:

Together the members of each staff made a group which they valued because it gave them a feeling of belonging. At the same time, they accepted a collective responsibility for the work of the school, so creating a strong team in which people helped, encouraged and substituted for one another (p. 58).

Second, interdependence was valued in the sense of working as a team. The collective responsibility on which teams were built showed itself in how everyone advised, supported, and helped one another. In one teacher's words: "If you say 'I'm doing such and such, I haven't got any good ideas', there will be six or seven different ideas thrown at you instantly." (p. 60).

Collaborative cultures, defined in terms of these values, make it more not less likely that diversity will be appreciated and accessible, while at the same time fostering interdependence as people learn from each other, identify common concerns, and work jointly on solving problems. Developing these cultures is not easy. As Nias et al. argue, they need a high degree of both security and openness among their teachers to work well. Collaborative cultures are very clearly sophisticated, and delicately balanced organizations, which is why they are so hard to achieve and even harder to maintain.

In closing this section, there are two other features of collaborative cultures which should be highlighted, because they figure so prominently in the guidelines and strategies for improvement formulated in Chapter 4. These are the role of *leadership*, and the relationship of collaborative schools to their *environments*.

*What's Worth Fighting For in the Principalship?* was devoted to an analysis of the principalship, and we will not attempt to repeat it here. We do, however, want to say three things about school leadership. First, the development of collaborative schools where they do exist has depended heavily on the actions of the principals in those schools (Fullan, 1991, Nias et al., 1989, Leithwood & Jantzi, 1990). Second, it is a particular *kind of leadership* that counts. It is not the charismatic, innovative high flyer that moves whole school cultures forward. Rather it is a more subtle kind of leadership which makes activity meaningful for others. Leading the development of collaborative schools in which teachers are enabled or empowered "to frame problems, and to discuss and work individually and collectively to understand and to change the situations that caused these problems" (Smyth, 1989: 190-1) is the basic role of school leadership as we see it. We will say more in chapter 4 about how principals can develop such collaborative schools.

The third and even more fundamental point is the reminder that leadership can and should come from a variety of sources in the school. In the fully functioning collaborative school, many (indeed all) teachers are leaders. In the long run, if the culture of collaborative schools becomes as firmly institutionalized as the current culture of individualism, schools will no longer need principals as we now know them.

The relationship of the school to the wider environment is also taken up in chapter 4. Here we have a few basic points to make. Collaborative schools are highly plugged into their environments—the local community, the regional, provincial and even national and international contexts. It is possible to become collaborative despite the environment, but it is not possible to stay collaborative without active involvement in and support from the environment.

# In the fully functioning collaborative school, many (indeed all) teachers are leaders.

There are at least two reasons why this is the case. First, in the same way that openness is necessary within the school, it also must characterize how the school connects with the outside. New ideas, better practices elsewhere, stimulation, pressure to take into account societal needs, and dissemination; (or what one has to offer to other teachers and schools) are all part of the spiritual vitality of collaborative schools. Nor can schools succeed if they do not establish close working relationships with parents and the community. Second, decisions outside the school obviously affect its future (such as how the new generation of teachers are trained, who is hired, who is moved and so on). We are not naive enough to suggest that these factors are controllable by the individual school, but it should also be clear that the collaborative school—to protect itself, to get even better—must constantly engage in and *negotiate* its future with the outside.

In sum, in addition to the values identified by Nias et al., collaborative cultures are also explicitly committed to continuous improvement, to searching out ways of improving practice whether these be found inside or outside the school.

## The Problem of Collaboration

Schools are hurting. Working together has never been more needed. Collaboration is an automatically attractive concept. This is the stuff of change, but also of failed solutions. We have also seen that the changes involved in moving toward effective collaboration are deep and complex. The mere existence of collaboration should not be mistaken for a thoroughgoing *culture* of it. Some kinds of collaboration are best avoided. Others are wastes of time and limited in their impact. Still others should be regarded only as way-stations to be surpassed in the pursuit of more ambitious forms. We examine three of these other forms of collaboration of which we should be more watchful: balkanization, comfortable collaboration, and contrived collegiality.

## 1.   Balkanization

In some schools, while teachers associate more closely with some of their colleagues than they do in a culture of individualism, they do so in particular groups more than in the school as a whole. Such schools have what might be called a *balkanized* teacher culture — a culture made up of separate and sometimes competing groups, jockeying for position and supremacy like loosely connected, independent city states.

Teachers in balkanized cultures attach their loyalties and identities to particular groups of their colleagues. These are usually colleagues with whom they work most closely, spend most time, socialize most often in the staffroom. The existence of such groups in a school often reflects and reinforces very different group outlooks on learning, teaching styles, discipline and curriculum. Balkanized cliques are not confined to conservative teachers. Groups of innovative teachers, who see themselves as ahead of their colleagues, can also segment themselves in ways that are detrimental to whole school development.

Balkanization may lead to poor communication, indifference, or groups going their separate ways in a school. This in turn can produce poor continuity in monitoring student progress and inconsistent expectations for their performance and behaviour. As Ball (1987) notes, it may generate squabbles and conflicts over space (room allocations, storage space), time (priority in scheduling) and resources (budgets, student numbers etc.,). The urgency and necessity of defending territory and status against claims from other groups explains the great seriousness and importance teachers attach to apparently "petty" disputes over things like rights to shelf and cupboard space in a school corridor (Hargreaves et al., 1988).

Balkanized cultures are a familiar feature of high-school life, mainly because of the strong subject-department structures on which high schools are based, but they can be found in elementary schools, as well. The most common form of balkanization in elementary schools arises from the separation of teachers into different divisions — primary, junior and intermediate. In a collaboratively-inclined school board, as we have seen in the recent investigation into preparation time, there were many instances of co-operation and joint planning among teachers within particular grades and divisions. Preparation time was often scheduled to encourage this, by same-grade teachers being released at the same time. And teachers who were involved in planning closely with their grade partners, generally spoke positively about the value of doing so. But regular co-operation across grades and divisions was a comparative rarity. Other research shows similar findings: elementary teachers consult much more often with same-grade and same division teachers than with other colleagues (Hargreaves, 1986). This grade-based insulation means that while commendable attention is often given to lateral curriculum coherence within grades and divisions, vertical continuity from one division, or sometimes even one grade to the next can be disconcertingly weak.

Thus, even the existence of innovation-oriented sub-groups such as those found in team teaching or peer coaching may or may not reflect an underlying collaborative culture in the school as a whole. In fact, Nias and her colleagues observed that like-minded teachers often cluster in subgroups that "impede school-wide acceptance of particular practices and inhibit the open discussion that might eventually lead to the creation of a whole-school perspective" (p. 53). We do not deny that teaming up with an innovative colleague can be a major step forward, but it is only a beginning.

Curriculum continuity and coordination across grades is far more likely in cultures that value individuals and their interactions with a variety of people across the school. Formal curriculum guidelines and administrative structures (like school improvement teams) by themselves do not result in curriculum coherence at the level of practice. Ultimately, effective continuity is secured more through human understanding, communication and agreement at an informal level and the necessary openness, trust and support that come with that. It is also a matter of creating a community of teachers whose experiences and commitments are not confined exclusively to a single grade, division or subject, but extend to the school as a whole. All this helps avoid unnecessary gaps or duplications in students' learning as they move from one grade to the next.

We are not saying that organizational arrangements are unimportant. They are essential to providing mechanisms and possibilities for working together (see Chapter 4). But we are saying that interpersonal rapport is the subframe that holds the formal business of curriculum continuity together. Without it, formal consultancy procedures are but a brittle administrative shell.

Some principals are keenly aware of the dangers of balkanization and have developed policies to counter its negative effects. These include:

- Preparation time arrangements, which give intermediate teachers covering for primary and junior classes an appreciative sense of the difficulties and skills involved in teaching younger children. This helps them develop appreciation of their colleagues' expertise.
- Temporary exchange of teachers for days, a few weeks or even a year between secondary school and the intermediate years of one of its "feeder" schools. This can promote greater understanding and continuity in meeting the needs of the transition years (Hargreaves and Earl, 1990).
- Arrangements for cross-grouping, involving teachers and students from different grades working together, can be particularly valuable

in softening the effects of balkanization and creating more under-standing among teachers who normally remain relatively isolated from one another.

These arrangements reaffirm two central principles that underpin collaborative staff relationships. First, routine experience of working with others provides a better route to understanding and cooperation than either rational persuasion to consider other teachers' viewpoints, or for-mal procedures to bring about closer liaison (through better record-keep-ing systems, for instance.) Second, teacher development is inseparable from curriculum development. These two areas of reform should be worked together in harness, not approached in isolation.

## Effective collaborations operate in the world of ideas, examining existing practices critically, seeking better alternatives and working hard together at bringing about improvements and assessing their worth.

### 2.   Comfortable Collaboration

Given the scarcity of collaborative cultures across school systems generally, their successful creation in at least some settings is a substan-tial achievement. However, as we noted earlier, collaboration often takes what we call bounded, rather than extended, forms. It can be bounded in the sense of not extending to classroom settings where teachers might be involved in joint teaching, mutual observation of one another's work, or action research. Even where teachers work together in preparation time, for instance, it is unusual for them to spend it in each other's classrooms. This restricts the extent to which teachers can inquire into and advise one another about their practice. It keeps some of the tougher questions about their work and how to improve it off the agenda. Major elements of the prevailing norms of privacy are left intact. A major challenge for schools is how to extend their collaborative work in this action-centred, class-room-based sense.

Bounded collaboration rarely reaches deep down to the grounds, the principles or the ethics of practice. It can get stuck with the more com-fortable business of advice-giving, trick-trading and material-sharing of a more immediate, specific and technical nature. Such collaboration does not extend beyond particular units of work or subjects of study to the wider purpose and value of what is taught and how. It is collaboration which focuses on the immediate, the short-term and the practical to the exclusion of longer-term planning concerns. It is collaboration which does not embrace the principles of systematic reflective practice. In the prep time study, even within the most collaborative settings, there was much talk of sharing, exchanging, coordinating, celebrating and supporting. But there was virtually no talk at all about inquiring, questioning, reflecting, criticizing and engaging in dialogue as positive and worthwhile activities. Research on site-based management also shows little evidence that this sort of collaboration results in instructional improvement in classrooms (Levine and Eubanks, 1989). It often remains at "the comfortable" level.

A further example is provided by Acker (1989), in her case studies of two primary schools in England and the ways in which they responded to the introduction of an externally-imposed National Curriculum. One of these schools had many of the apparent characteristics of collaboration - high participation in decision-making, blurring of staff roles, caring, warmth, humour, camaraderie and gratitude. As well as the usually mentioned upsides to this culture of collaboration, Acker's study identified a number of difficulties. Some of these difficulties were eventually resolved by the school, but they do point to some of the key problems of collaboration:

- the accustomed way of working was "casual, flexible and warm rather than organized and efficient".
- collaborative decisions were taken even on minor matters which consumed a great deal of time.
- roles were so blurred that when external innovations needed to be addressed, resources were late being put in place because no one was clearly responsible for them.
- staff relied on memory, on an oral tradition rather than on written records when making decisions. This led to a lack of clarity and collective certainty about school policy.
- the staff had little contact with theory, ideas or professional advice outside the school and relied perhaps too heavily on the headteacher (principal) for this.
- the school tended to be reactive rather than proactive with regard to external changes that might affect the school.
- discussions and decisions about fast-tracked, externally imposed innovations tended to be protracted and often unfocused - leading to disconcerting delays in the implementation of policy.

Strong collaborative schools are not soft and unfocused. They do not act as if the world outside is an annoyance. In this school, and in many like it, there is perhaps too much emphasis on sharing and celebrating experience, and not enough on inquiring into and extending it beyond the walls of the school. Collegiality shouldn't stop at congeniality. It is all too easy to avoid searching discussions and joint work which might expose disagreements on the principles and practice of teaching. This kind of collaboration is too cosy.

Effective collaboration is not always easy. It brings with it a measure of difficulty and even of discomfort on occasion. Warm, cosy relationships and an atmosphere of trust and openness are almost certainly necessary to supply a basis of security on which these more challenging processes of inquiry can be developed. But to bite the bullet of fundamental, deep and lasting change, improvement efforts should move beyond cooperative decision-making and planning, sharing experience and resources, and supportive interpersonal relationships into joint work, mutual observation, and focused reflective inquiry. Effective collaborations operate in the world of ideas, examining existing practices critically, seeking better alternatives and working hard together at bringing about improvements and assessing their worth. We believe this to be one of the key challenges for collaborative working and professional development in the future.

## 3. Contrived Collegiality

# Building collaborative cultures involves a long developmental journey. There are no easy short cuts.

Because collaborative cultures do not evolve quickly, they can be unattractive to administrators looking for swift implementation expedients. Collaborative cultures are difficult to pin down in time and space, living as they do mainly in the interstices of school life. Collaborative cultures are also unpredictable in their consequences. The curriculum that will be developed, the learning that will be fostered, the goals that will be formulated- these things cannot always be predicted confidently beforehand.

For some administrators, this unpredictability can be disconcerting. What is fostered, formulated and developed by these collaborative cultures may not always correspond with administrators' own preferred purposes or current board priorities. This might explain why most collaborative cultures take the bounded form, where the grounds of practice, of curriculum and instruction, are not investigated in a searching way, on a continuous basis, across the school community. More extended forms of collaboration of this sort almost certainly require formal devolution of responsibility for much curriculum development, for something significant for teachers to collaborate about, to schools and teachers themselves.

The unpredictability of collaborative cultures can also lead administrators toward forms of collegiality which they can control, regulate, or tame. These more controlled approaches toward collaboration, we call *contrived collegiality* (Hargreaves, 1989). Contrived collegiality is characterized by a set of formal, specific, bureaucratic procedures to increase the attention being given to joint teacher planning, consultation and other forms of working together. It can be seen in initiatives such as peer coaching, mentor schemes, joint planning in specially provided rooms, site-based management, formally scheduled meetings and clear job descriptions and training programs for those in consultative roles. These sorts of initiatives are administrative contrivances designed to get collegiality going in schools where little has existed before. They are meant to encourage greater association among teachers and to foster more sharing, learning and improvement of skills and expertise. Contrived collegiality is also meant to assist the successful implementation of new approaches and techniques from the outside into a more responsive and supportive school culture.

Contrived collegiality is double-edged. It has both positive and negative possibilities depending on how and when it is used. At its best, contrived collegiality can be a useful preliminary phase in setting up more enduring collaborative relationships between teachers. It is a way of putting teachers in touch. Principals can then build on those informal elements of recognition, trust and support which are essential to creating an effective teaching community. Some contrivance is necessary in the establishment of virtually all collaborative cultures. They don't happen by themselves. Shrewd scheduling, releasing people to have the opportunity to plan together, principals themselves providing cover to facilitate such planning, instigating arrangements for teachers to consult with teacher librarians and with special education resource teachers — all these things help create, but do not, of course, guarantee appropriate conditions for collaborative cultures to develop. Contrived collegiality can also disturb collective complacency, and extend what it is that teachers collaborate about. It can add focus to joint work.

At its worst, though, contrived collegiality can be reduced to a quick, slick administrative surrogate for collaborative teacher cultures. Such cultures take much more time, care and sensitivity to build than speedily implemented changes of an administratively superficial nature. If done badly, contrived collegiality can *reduce* teachers motivation to cooperate further. Building collaborative cultures involves a long developmental journey. There are no easy short cuts.

Of course, as we have argued, collaborative cultures do not arise spontaneously or completely by themselves. They, too, require managerial guidance and intervention. But, broadly speaking, this is intervention which is supportive and facilitating, which creates opportunities for teachers to work together in school time. Collaborative cultures do not mandate collegial support and partnership: they foster and facilitate it. This is what distinguishes them from schools characterized by more superficial versions of contrived collegiality.

In some of the most questionable forms of contrived collegiality, colleagueship and partnership are administratively imposed, creating a degree of inflexibility that violates those principles of discretionary judgement which make up the core of teacher professionalism. There are many examples of imposed collegiality which deceptively sail under the flag of collaborative culture. Certain kinds of peer coaching relationships which don't just encourage but actually mandate teachers to work together on improvements to their practice, amount to imposed collegiality. (Hargreaves and Dawe 1990). Compulsory forms of clinical supervision where assistance is bound up with evaluation, and where help is offered under the canopy of hierarchy, amount to another kind of imposed collegiality (Grimmett and Crehan, 1991). Requiring that classroom teachers always meet with their special education resource teacher at a regularly assigned time, even when there is no business to discuss, is yet another instance of imposed collegiality (Hargreaves, forthcoming).

Preparation time use is a further example. Interview responses from some teachers in the preparation time study indicated that while they would normally use preparation periods for collaborative purposes designated by their principal, in a proportion of them, they would retreat to their own room or other space, to work alone, for their own classes, clearing away the plethora of little tasks for which preparation time has such importance. Yet, in doing so, they would feel guilty, fearful of discovery by their principal, and not without justification. One principal explained to us how infuriated he was when he discovered that teachers he had personally covered so they could be released to plan together, were, on the occasion he checked up on them, not planning together at all but working, preparing and marking alone. In response, the teachers concerned asked him to trust them. They had been planning together, they said, but just then it was more appropriate for them to work alone. The principal was neither convinced nor mollified. Having invested so much of his own time to allow them to plan together, he felt his trust had been abused when they did not.

Preparation time use, and what may be an appropriate use of such time, has complicated relationships to teachers' lives and work which principals cannot always see. For instance, most teachers interviewed in the study did not see planning time, as it was sometimes called, as the best time to plan at all. Preparation time periods were usually fairly short — 40 minutes or less. Many minutes were often lost looking after classes until the covering teacher arrived, taking children to the gym and supervising them getting changed, walking across to the staffroom if the teacher's own classroom was in use, and so on. This time was commonly regarded as too short for sustained planning, be it collective or individual. These teachers preferred to plan at other times, such as lunch or after school. Preparation time was used more to "clear the decks" of the innumerable, small tasks like photocopying and telephoning that could be dispatched less efficiently at other times when other teachers would be clamouring for the same resources. This pattern of work in preparation time was highly useful for many teachers and freed up their time to plan in a more sustained way at other points in the school day.

For other teachers, however, preparation time was ideal for planning with colleagues. Coaching and refereeing sports teams, for instance, gave some teachers little opportunity to meet with colleagues at other times. Pressing domestic responsibilities made it difficult for a number of women teachers to stay long after school and thereby to be able to plan with colleagues then (although some went to extraordinary inconvenience to do so). Preparation time for them was a good time to work with colleagues.

Preparation time and its uses therefore have a complicated and variable relationship to teachers' work and life circumstances. There is no unambiguous administrative formula for dealing with this. The important principle, rather, is administrative flexibility and discretion in delegating decisions about how preparation time periods are to be used, to teachers themselves. Overall it is better that principals set expectations for collegial *tasks* (through discussion and development with teachers), rather than expectations for collegial *time*. Over-managing collegiality is something to avoid.

One last point is worth making in examining collaborative cultures. Reviewing the research on collaboratively run organizations, Rothschild (1990) concludes that women's socialization prepares them better to

60

develop and lead such organizations. Women tend, more than men, to negotiate conflict in ways that protect ongoing working relationships (as compared to seeing conflict in win-lose terms), and they tend to value relationships in and of themselves as part of their commitment to care (rather than seeing relationships as instrumental to other purposes). Shakeshaft (1987) finds similar patterns in her studies of women and leadership in school systems.

This does not mean that all women teachers make better principals than men teachers. There are good and bad principals of both sexes. And it does not mean that these characteristics are fixed at birth. But the patterns are evident. As more women move into senior positions, our models and understanding of effective leadership may undergo significant transformations. It will be important to seek, appreciate and foster new forms of collaboration. We must also learn from and integrate more stereotypically masculine qualities of task orientation and analysis if we are to move collaborative work into the domain of rigorous inquiry and improvement. One reason why women's forms of leadership are especially important is that the presence of women administrators, at least in numbers, is relatively new. There is also some evidence that more gender-balanced groups improve the performance of both men and women (Rothschild, 1990).

The point is not to fix men and women into stereotypes, but to identify the most powerful and enduring qualities of collaborative leadership, to foster them in teachers and administrators of both sexes, and to build effective leadership teams where these qualities are shared and combined across groups. This is an enormously difficult challenge because we do not yet know how best to develop and sustain collaborative cultures over long periods of time. Because of this difficulty, contrived collegiality is likely to characterize many of our early attempts. When it is used in a facilitative, not a controlling way, contrived collegiality can provide a starting point, and a necessary first step toward building collaborative cultures with focus and depth. It cannot, however, provide an expediential substitute for those cultures themselves, because they take time, patience, and skill to evolve and develop.

## Conclusion

We have seen that collaborative cultures are highly sophisticated. They cannot be created overnight. Many forms of collegiality are superficial, partial, and even counter productive. It is not possible to have strong collaborative cultures without strong individual development. We must avoid crushing individuality in the drive to eliminate individualism. At the same time, teachers should not be left completely alone or leave each other alone. The stimulation and pressure from in-built interactive professionalism serves as a constant source of new ideas and support, as well as a form of accountability more suitable to the high discretion, and high energy profession of teaching. What we can do to move forward with this vision is the subject of chapter 4.

## Many forms of collegiality are suferficial, partial, and even counterproductive.

# Chapter 4

# Interactive Professionalism
# and Guidelines For Action

## There can be no improvement without the teacher.

The greatest problem in teaching is not how to get rid of the "deadwood", but how to create, sustain and motivate good teachers throughout their careers. Interactive professionalism is the key to this. For us it entails:

- discretionary judgement as the heart of professionalism.
- collaborative work cultures.
- norms of continuous improvement where new ideas are sought inside and outside one's setting.
- reflection in, on and about practice in which individual and personal development is honoured, along with collective development and assessment.
- greater mastery, efficacy and satisfaction in the profession of teaching.

Interactive professionalism involves redefining the role of teachers and the conditions in which they work. We have implied directions and guidelines for action throughout the monograph, but we highlight the main themes here. These recommendations are cast as guidelines for action rather than as specific techniques, for two reasons. First, the main purpose is to develop a different *mindset* to the problems we identified in Chapter 1. There are plenty of specific strategies and techniques available, but they fail, or enjoy only short term success, unless they result in new ways of thinking and acting that permeate the daily life of schools.

Second, we can never know what specific solutions are desirable, possible or efficacious for the many different situations that teachers face. Teaching cannot be standarized. It is through informed experiments, pursuing promising directions, and testing out and refining new arrangements and practices that we will make the most headway. Therefore, *action* in trying out new approaches is imperative.

We do refer to particular techniques and methods. But guidelines imbued with a new mindset and a bias for action are more likely to generate solutions that work and that last. We start with guidelines for teachers because we consider these to be the foundation for any long term solution. There are more teachers than principals, and more principals than school board administrators. We want to put the power of possibility into the hands of this majority. We then consider what principals can do to facilitate and propel interactive, professional school cultures. Finally, we have some recommendations for how those outside the school can contribute to teacher and school development.

## Guidelines For Teachers

Twelve guidelines for teachers can be suggested. These guidelines will not be effective in isolation from each other — they must be practised together, in combinations. They complement and build on each other. However, as before, each individual must find his or her particular configuration of satisfaction, and must be prepared to vary and adapt it according to personal and organizational circumstances. The guidelines are:

1. Locate, listen to and articulate your inner voice.
2. Practise reflection in action, on action and about action.
3. Develop a risk-taking mentality.
4. Trust processes as well as people.
5. Appreciate the total person in working with others.
6. Commit to working with colleagues.
7. Seek variety and avoid balkanization.
8. Redefine your role to extend beyond the classroom.
9. Balance work and life.
10. Push and support principals and other administrators to develop interactive professionalism.
11. Commit to continuous improvement and perpetual learning.
12. Monitor and strengthen the connection between your development and students' development.

Although we advocate starting with yourself, we predict that together with accompanying and ensuing changes in the context of teaching, the results of practising all twelve guidelines will be cumulative and contagious. Once mobilized, these and our other guidelines will produce more fundamental and effective change than existing reform strategies do. In each case, we will clarify the meaning of the guideline and refer to techniques for following it.

64

## 1.  Locate, Listen To and Articulate Your Inner Voice

Recall our discussion in Chapter 1 of the importance of individuality, and the role of personal time and solitude in developing one's values and ideas. With Storr (1988: 28), we noted how, in the rapid-paced environments of modern society, we can easily become alienated from our deepest needs and feelings. Classroom teaching is, by its very nature, rapid-paced. In Philip Jackson's (1968) terms, it has a "pressing immediacy" about it. There are always things to be done, decisions to be made, children's needs to be met, not just every day, but every minute, every second. This is the stuff of teaching. There is no let-up. The energy, activity and judgement this immediacy calls for can be a source of immense stimulation and satisfaction for many teachers. But for others, the constant pressure can be more enervating than energizing. Over time, it can erode one's personal resources. And it can make it difficult to look more deeply and widely beyond the here and now. In the rush of events, and in the face of overload, there never seems to be time to reflect, to take stock, to check out what we are really doing and why. Pressure precludes time to reflect. Lack of reflection obscures ways to relieve the pressure. The cycle is a vicious one.

Some of this is a problem with the system. Work pressures *have* intensified over the years. Innovations and inservices have multiplied. Paperwork and form-filling have proliferated. The problem of overload and insufficient time is not an imaginary one. Something *does* have to be done about the conditions of teaching and we will address this later. But time and resources — the traditional collective bargaining issues — are not enough. Preparation time, we have seen, does not itself guarantee teacher collaboration. Commitment and will are also needed. Some of this commitment must come from administrators. But teachers must be committed too.

Teachers must want to reflect and reflect deeply. They must believe it is important to get in touch with their feelings and purposes. And they must be prepared to put other things, even important things, aside to do it. It's a matter of the tortoise and the hare. Sometimes, the marking, the bulletin board or that extra resource item should wait, because a little time for reflection will lead to better things in the long run.

Often, when we say we have no time for something, it's an evasion. What we mean is we have more immediate or convenient things to do with that time. Of course, bulletin boards and visual aids are important. But doing them doesn't make you feel personally uncomfortable. It isn't disquieting. It isn't a personal challenge. Listening to our inner voice is. It requires not just time, but courage and commitment too. Having the courage and commitment to reflect means putting other things aside to do it.

How many times have we seen an unacceptable, even atrocious situation persist even though the majority of people in that situation individually oppose it without explicitly confronting their own views? How often do we allow injustice to continue because we are afraid to speak up, or think no one will listen? How often, for instance, do we allow the hard and hectoring teacher to continue humiliating and verbally abusing students because the good and the kind people stand by and say nothing? And how often do we turn away from the discomforting voice inside us that says we may not be serving all our students as well as we might, that we might be challenging the more able while giving the less able a blander diet of basic skills, or that we might be involving and questioning the boys in class more than the girls or vice-versa.

This guideline has very much to do with getting in touch with our own personal values and sources of energy and purpose; with what David Hunt (1987, forthcoming), calls "beginning with ourselves". Hunt asks how we would describe our present energy level:

- enthusiastic or empty?
- buoyant or bored?
- exhuberant or flat?
- bursting or lethargic?

If we frequently experience the feelings embodied in the left column it is likely that we are resonating with our inner voice. If not, we need to do something to activate what is meaningful and energizing in our lives.

Teachers have strong values about doing work that makes a difference. Because of overload and the rush of daily events, we often neglect our basic values. Guideline 1 suggests that we must ask and remind ourselves what values and goals are most important, what frustrates us most, and what we stand for. Locating and articulating our inner voice provide great sources of clarity and energy for transcending overload. The morality and practicality of improvement require that teachers locate this inner voice, that they listen to it seriously, and that they articulate it so as to make its power felt among their colleagues.

We hope it is clear in all our guidelines that we are not recommending that teachers become introspective hermits. Indeed, sharing and interaction is vital to identifying, developing and acting upon our own inner voices. But private time and private thinking are also vital to keep us honest and alive. One thing worth fighting for, then, especially since it is so very neglected, is the time, the courage, and the commitment to reach into our own inner selves; to locate, develop and articulate our purpose and our voice.

> When from our better selves, we have too long
> Been parted by the hurrying world, and droop,
> Sick of its business, of its pleasures tired,
> How gracious, how benign, is Solitude.
>     (Wordsworth, *The Prelude,* cited by Storr, 1988)

## 2.   Reflection In, On and About Action

Reflection in, on and about action is an extension of our first guideline, but is more specific and action-oriented. The essence of Guideline 2 is to make our thinking about action more explicit through a continuous process of reflection in, on and about experiences or practices in which we are engaged.

The concept of "reflective practitioner" has been pioneered by Donald Schon (1987), as a way of describing and developing skilled and thoughtful judgement in professions like teaching. It has quickly gained popularity in education as a rationale for moving teacher educators and staff developers beyond mindsets focused on rather narrow forms of training, to ones embracing wider processes of thoughtful education — not just in the sense of ivory-towered contemplation, but in ways that link reflection directly to practice (e.g. Grimmett and Erickson, 1988).

But alongside these positive developments have emerged some dangers and confusions as well. In many cases "reflective practice" has become a buzz-word or slogan. Sometimes, virtually any act of thinking has been hailed as embodying the principles of reflective practice. Because of this, the rhetoric of reflective practice has sometimes been used to dress up what we already do in new language, instead of inspiring us to do something different and better. Thinking is nothing new. Deeper reflection that leads to new insights and improvements in practices is rarer.

As a slogan, reflective practice is like collaboration. While presented as having a single, agreed-upon meaning, in reality, it has many. There are weak forms of reflection as well as strong ones. To talk about them as if they are all the same is misleading. When we advocate teacher reflection, we should therefore do so clearly and wisely, not glibly. The key questions we need to pose are what kinds of reflection are there and what can they help us do? The vast majority of teachers do reflect in some fashion in and on their practice. But this sense of reflective practice is a weak one. Stronger versions of a more searching kind that lead to more profound improvements are in much shorter supply. There are three missing dimensions to many teachers' reflective practice that deserve some attention here.

First, when teachers reflect in and on their practice, they usually do so with limited data. Most of their evidence on how they are doing and how they have done is based on their own personal impressions gathered in the busy and often frenetic happenings of classroom life. While such judgements and impressions are certainly helpful, they are not a sufficient basis for improvement. Teachers could, for example, make more effective use of feedback from their students. Students are a great and underrated source of teacher development (Thiessen, 1991). If we collected evidence more thoroughly from students, we would get better clues about what and how to improve. There are many ways to do this other than through personal impressions and test scores. Teachers can get more extensive feedback through the use of student journals; through systematic evaluations of courses or units of work; through individual or group discussions after courses of study; and through efforts to involve students directly in the process of innovation (Hargreaves, 1989, Rudduck, 1991). Thorough and effective monitoring of student development can be a powerful spur to teacher development. The reverse is also true: student development benefits in turn from the improvement and risk-taking that constitutes teacher development.

This brings us to our second point. Even with good feedback from students, relying on our own classroom experience is not usually enough to provoke stronger and deeper kinds of reflection. Our own experience is partial. Deeper reflection requires other eyes, other perspectives as well as our own. Part of the power of collaboration is the way it can bring other perspectives to bear on our own work. Peer coaching, team teaching, classroom observation, and even some kinds of performance appraisal can be a real stimulus to searching reflection. So, too, can collaborative inquiry outside the classroom — for example, in collaborative planning, teacher support groups and professional dialogue. While reflection in and on action will often require moments of solitude, other colleagues will also need to be involved if reflection is to be deepened and extended into those areas of discomfort and dissonance that precipitate change by exposing the gaps between what we think we do and what we really do.

A third missing dimension concerns "critical reflection about purpose and context" (Louden, 1991). Reflective practice can often get restricted to low-level technical concerns, to issues of what works and what doesn't. These are important, but they are not the whole story. Sometimes, we also need to review the purposes and principles that underpin our classroom judgements, our reflections in action. We need to review, for instance, not just whether our questioning strategies keep students on task and in order, ie. whether they "work" in this practical sense. We also need to review whether they develop higher order as well as lower order thinking skills, whether they favour "more able" over "less able" students, or whether they involve boys more than girls etc. We need to reflect about these ethics and principles in our actions. We need to reflect *about* action, that is, as well as in it and on it.

This means reflecting about our purposes, as we have said. It also means reflecting about the context of our teaching in terms of how it helps or hinders us in realizing those purposes. If we confront the fact that our context may be preventing us from fulfilling our purposes, or that we may have drifted into complying with institutional demands of which we disapprove, this more fundamental kind of reflection can propel us into doing something to change the context of our work, so our teaching can be more authentic. This may mean working through the teacher federations for better working conditions. Or it may mean working together with your principal to get him or her to make decisions more collaboratively. It may mean many things. But the important point is to focus reflection not only on one's own classroom, but also on the things that directly and indirectly affect the classroom, and to use this focus as a springboard for action.

There are many techniques for developing strong forms of reflective practice and we will list a few of them now. These are presented not as an inflexible mandate, but as an open-ended menu of possibilities. Some of the techniques we list, like teacher research, take a great deal of time and are not suited to all teachers. Others, for example, ones that involve a great deal of writing in diaries and journals, may suit only the more literary and introspective among us. But the possibilities listed contain a wide variety of options that offer something for most teachers. We refer to seven here:

- **Evoking Positive Personal Images**
Block (1987: 123-4) advocates focusing on an important project, probing "why" it is so important to you, thereby getting at deeper goals and values. Hunt (forthcoming) says that by recalling and dwelling on positive experiences we can release energy within us. This potential is not unlimited, of course. Some work environments are so disempowering, some leaders so power-hungry and obstinate, that exit from the organization may be the only positive strategy available. But even this is a constructive choice - better than drifting aimlessly and dispiritingly along in

69

an unsatisfactory situation. More often, personal reflection of the kind advocated by Block and Hunt will suggest that exit is not the only option and that positive strategies to improve the environment are feasible. Pausing to reflect, in a positive way, is the first step here.

- **Professional Reading**

    This can give rapid access to other perspectives and ideas on new programs, new teaching techniques, ways to work with colleagues and general possibilities for improvement. Such reading need not involve daunting encounters with esoteric, technical jargon. Many professional magazines are user-friendly, and present succinct, up-to-date and readable accounts of educational research in ways that are valuable for teachers. Teachers often complain there isn't time for professional reading. But just one hour for one article a week gives access to at least four new ideas and insights a month. Is it really time or is it priorities that are at stake here? Don't hope you'll get to your reading sometime by fitting it around all the other things you already do. Schedule in a regular timeslot and protect it. Stick with this strategy for a few weeks at least and see what you gain in understanding, insight and fresh perspective as a result. Share some of the articles with your colleagues. Leave copies of interesting pieces in the staffroom. Put one in your principal's mailbox. Get access to the knowledge base and try to share it with your colleagues.

- **Professional Dialogue**

    Shared reading can be a stimulus for professional talk about new strategies and ways to improve. Such professional dialogue extends beyond practical tips and moral support. It is specific and focuses on action. At the same time, it connects with inquiry and existing knowledge bases. Professional dialogue uses research to raise questions about practice. But the research is not invulnerable. Practice can be used to raise questions about the research too.

    Richardson and Anders (1990) describe a specific example of this process as it applies to reading practices. Their method has teachers describe and examine their explanations for their present practices in teaching reading, while juxtaposing these with premises derived from research. The intent is not to have teachers conform to the research findings, but to make their own empirical and value premises more explicit by comparing them with those of other teachers and of research. By examining their practices and by critically reflecting on the reasons for them, teachers push themselves to give good reasons for what they are doing. This in turn prompts them to change their practice when they find it wanting.

- **Teacher Support Groups**

Teacher support groups within and across schools can give a focus for professional improvement in an informal and supportive environment. One advantage of teacher support groups is that they are developed by teachers themselves, not laid on by administrators. Indeed, the confidence and creativity generated in some support groups can lead teachers to resist simplistically-conceived changes mandated from the outside in favour of their own improvements. Many teacher support groups have started quite informally, with two or three teachers meeting once a month in a restaurant, for instance. The purpose of such meetings is not just to chat. It is to talk professionally about improvements, and to make some changes in practice.

Such support groups often grow in numbers and in the scope of their influence. Some have even led to newsletters, professional publication, teaching materials, teacher centres, inservices for other teachers and national conferences. The advantages of teacher support groups are twofold. They have a strong social dimension, and they also extend beyond it. They are developed by teachers, with teachers and for teachers.

- **Teacher Research**

Teacher research, especially action research, can be a particularly effective way to link improvement and inquiry to classroom practice (Kemmis and McTaggart, 1988, Oja and Smulyan, 1989). Professional researchers don't have a monopoly on research. Teachers can do it too. While this work can be time-consuming and demanding and is probably not viable as a system-wide or even school-wide change, some teachers find it an excellent strategy for improvement which they themselves control. Teacher research can take many forms and use many resources. Lytle and Cochran-Smith (1990) provide several examples including the use of teacher journals, teacher essays, and classroom inquiry in which two or more teachers conduct small scale studies on particular questions.

- **Autobiographies and Life Histories**

If our teaching is grounded in our purposes, the kinds of experiences we have had, and the kinds of people we have become, one way to retrieve the grounds of our teaching is to write personal autobiographies or life histories of our growth and development as teachers. Writing and studying these autobiographies or narratives of our experience can provide excellent opportunities for personal reflection, for reexamining our purposes, and for identifying how we can and want to change (Goodson

71

1991; Connelly and Clandinin, 1988, Raymond, Butt and Townsend, 1991).

Sharing autobiographies with other teachers can provide an audience and stimulus for writing and also sources of questioning and interpretation that probe the writers to reflect more deeply on their motivations and purposes. By writing and sharing such autobiographies the writer runs risks of personal exposure and vulnerability. Often these risks may be too great to warrant sharing life histories with colleagues in one's own school. But trusted colleagues from other schools, perhaps even on courses, can sometimes provide a safer environment for this kind of reflection.

- **Courses and Advanced Qualifications**

Courses can themselves be a great spur to personal reflection. Not all reflection needs be school-based. Indeed, as we have just noted some of the most intellectually challenging and emotionally heart-searching kinds of reflection may require the time and safety of protected environments where inquiry and questioning are the legitimate focus of teacher activity (Oberg and Underwood, 1991). External courses can provide such environments. Not all do, and a number become reduced to the kind of hoop-jumping and paper-chasing that is the butt of teachers' stereotypes about their seemingly careerist colleagues. But many external courses really do stimulate rigorous reflection of a personally challenging nature. Many teachers already take external courses: up to a third of Ontario teachers at any one time, for instance (Fullan, Connelly and Watson, 1990). More could profitably do so. In the move toward more school-based teacher development, their value should not be underestimated.

### 3. Develop a Risk-Taking Mentality

We know that innovation and improvement are accompanied by anxiety and stress, especially at the early stages of renewal (Fullan, 1991). In other words, every time we take steps toward improvement, we are undertaking risks. So, taking risks is partly a matter of will.

Three general criteria for beginning to practise risk-taking are: be selective (try it with one or two things), do it on a small scale, and take a positive rather than a negative risk (take steps toward a positive vision, rather than refusing to do something).

Two examples congruent with other guidelines are:

72

- **Try Out A New Practice.** Teachers get exposed to countless new practices through professional development in the course of the year. Many will be being attempted in one's own school. Trying out a new practice is immediately risky. It is new for students as well as for the teacher. It requires skills, coordination and familiarity which are not acquired instantly. Take one of these new practices that appeals to you, and try it out on a small scale. Add a new teaching practice to your repertoire. (All the better, as we will suggest later, with at least one other teacher, but this is not essential).

- **Take the first-step** in acting on the other guidelines. For example in helping to establish collaborative work cultures (guideline 6), ask for help or assistance from a colleague, especially from someone with less experience than you; praise your principal; offer to be a mentor; offer to be observed in teaching (or to observe); and so on.

It is alright to fail, as long as you learn from it. Hunt says that having a sense of humour is intimately related to being comfortable with risk-taking. The question is, "can I accept my frailties and imperfections with good humour without losing the possibility of developing further?" (p. 126).

Once risk-taking gets rolling, we learn more from our new experience. The cumulative effect is a greater range of skills, and professional confidence. The willingness to take selective positive risks may be less risky than we think. In many situations, we may be all the more appreciated or respected for such actions. Even if we are not, whose problem is it? Listen to your inner voice.

## 4.   Trust Processes As Well As People

There is a reciprocal relationship between risk and trust (Giddens 1990). In simple societies, risk was associated with permanent danger, such as with threats of wild beasts, marauding raiders, famines and floods. Personal trust in family, friends and community helped people cope with these persistent risks. Risk in simple societies was something to be minimized or avoided. In modern organizations and societies, risk and trust take on different qualities. In modern schools, especially larger ones, there may be too many adults to know all of them well. Personnel may change frequently, including leaders. Trust in individuals is no longer sufficient. When key individuals leave and leaders move on, exclusive reliance on personal trust can cause massive instability. This is why innovative schools spearheaded by charismatic leaders often revert to mediocrity when they leave.

Another kind of trust is therefore called for in modern organizations like our schools: trust in processes. Trust in expertise and processes helps organizations develop and solve problems on a continuing basis in an environment where problems and challenges are continuous and changing. Processes to be trusted here are ones that maximize the organization's collective expertise and improve its problem-solving capacities. These include improved communication, shared decision-making, creation of opportunities for collegial learning, networking with outside environments, experimenting with new ideas and practices, commitment to continuous inquiry, and so on. Trust in people remains important, but trust in expertise and processes supersedes it. Trust in processes is open-ended, risky. But it is essential to learning and improvement.

This means that in modern schools, risk is something to be embraced rather than avoided. Risk-taking fosters learning, adaptability and improvement. The trust it presumes may need to extend beyond the close interpersonal understandings that make up the collaborative cultures we described earlier. These understandings and cultures are important, especially in smaller schools and teams. But larger and more rapidly changing schools require teachers who can invest trust in processes too, and who can trust their colleagues provisionally, even before they know them well. We are not advocating contrived collegiality here, which can substitute managerial tricks for organizational trust. But we are advocating a kind of trust that extends beyond the deep knowledge of interpersonal relationships. This trust in process and positive orientation to risk is something that teachers need to exercise, something we need to develop among our experienced teachers, and something we need to use as a criterion for selecting new ones.

## 5.  Appreciate the Total Person In Working With Others

Trust in process will often lead to trust in people. Trying to understand the people with whom we work is important for building these relationships. Appreciating the total person in our colleagues involves, by definition, both the professional and non-professional realms of life. We saw in Nias et al.'s (1989) case studies that "valuing individuals as people" was a strong feature of the collaborative schools. Interest in and consideration of the life circumstances of individual teachers are difficult because they mean balancing concern on the one hand, with respect for privacy on the other. Research on life-cycles, career cycles and gender factors in teaching all show how teachers' personal circumstances differ and vary over time (Huberman, 1991, Sikes, 1985, Krupp, 1989). If we do not relate appropriately to other people, we increase the chances of conflict, alienation and mismatched responses or strategies.

On the personal side, we can be more sensitive to the changing and current circumstances of others. We can appreciate others, sometimes by backing off, other times by showing praise and gratitude for jobs well done, and still other times by showing care and concern.

On the professional side, we can recognize that there are many legitimate routes to teacher development. For some, this involves participation in school-wide reform, and district leadership. For others, as Huberman (1991) so clearly argues, extending one's contact to a handful of colleagues, who are working on similar problems, and who are often outside one's school is more appropriate. And we know that different approaches are necessary for the beginning teacher and the mid-and later-career teacher. The point is not to accept the status quo, but to extend your teaching repertoire and opportunities for professional learning according to your professional and life circumstances.

## 6.   Commit To Working With Colleagues

# Be cautious of superficial and wasteful forms of collaboration, and of collaboration in the service of ends you regard as questionable, impractical or indefensible.

We argued in Chapter 3 that working with others is essential to school reform and individual development. Part of this guideline is to be cautious of superficial and wasteful forms of collaboration, and of collaboration in the service of ends you regard as questionable, impractical or indefensible. The other part is to begin working earnestly on developing and multiplying stronger forms of collegiality. There are any number of specific steps to take: plan a unit with a grade partner; engage in peer observation; work with a colleague on an improvement by trying out a promising new classroom practice in your subject area; invite the special education resource teacher or teacher-librarian to plan and try something new in your classroom; form a small study group (or support group) with a few colleagues, etc.

At the more institutional level, become involved in one of the many new collaborative projects being attempted: as a mentor for beginning teachers; in a peer coaching project (see Watson and Kilcher, 1990); as part of a school-improvement team; as part of a group implementing new teaching techniques; in a curriculum development project based on teacher collaboration; or in response to a principal, vice-principal or lead teacher inviting involvement. Institutionally sponsored projects have the advantage of legitimacy and resources.

Hunt (forthcoming) suggests four questions to achieve "the *synergy* of sharing": "Do I make time and opportunity for sharing? Do I listen to others in a way which is helpful to both of us? Do I present my views in ways which invite their being transformed and clarified? Do I respect another's privacy if they do not wish to share?" (p. 125). Sharing competence, and showing vulnerability can lead the way to opening up sharing by others.

The underlying goal, and one must explicitly work on this, is to build and nurture interactive professionalism and collaborative cultures. This means two things. First, individual instances of collegiality, as recommended above, do not by themselves represent values and norms of working together, openness, and the seeking of continuous improvements which reflect and generate multiple instances of collaboration. Second, and related, it takes a long time and a great deal of care to build collaborative work cultures. This is done through multiplying the number of small scale examples engaged in by more and more teachers within and across schools. When it becomes natural fare for the vast majority of teachers to seek and engage in professional exchanges and action, we will know that we are approaching collaborative work cultures.

## 7. Seek Variety and Avoid Balkanization

Guideline 7 is a refinement of the previous guideline. In chapter 3, we discussed the problem of balkanization or cliques of teachers keeping to themselves. We usually think of such teachers as groups of reactionaries. However, groups of innovators can also become compartmentalized into subcultures. Sometimes this is because they have been deliberately sealed off by their colleagues. At other times, it is because they pursue innovation in a manner that distances themselves from other teachers. The solution is to seek some *diversity* in collegial action, and to avoid becoming part of an exclusive "club". Switching classes; covering a very different grade in preparation time; participating in projects and other networks of professionals outside one's school; undertaking and using graduate work; and taking courses or workshops in educational leadership in order to become a more effective teacher-leader in your school are all examples of valuable extensions to collegiality.

In short, it is important to be sensitive to the whole culture of the school. If new to a school, take time to learn and appreciate the existing culture before questioning it. This rule applies to principals too. If certain others in your school do not seem interested in improvement, test out some possibilities before drawing conclusions.

It should also be emphasized that whole schools—innovative or traditional—can get balkanized vis-a-vis other schools and the system. This is a particularly serious problem where different "phases" or "panels" are concerned — where the relationships between elementary and secondary schools are particularly weak. There is considerable research to suggest that elementary and secondary teachers have highly stereotypical and inaccurate views of each other's practice (Hargreaves 1986, Hargreaves and Earl 1990). These stereotypes, like all stereotypes, feed off a combination of high emotion and low information. One of their unfortunate effects is that in their anxiety to prepare students for the rigours and requirements of high school, Grade 7 and 8 teachers often prepare them for an imagined world that is far tougher than the high schools that really exist. Intermediate teachers, as a result, often become stricter, more traditional and more content-centred than high school teachers themselves. They become more like high school teachers than high school teachers are (Tye, 1985)!

A key point for teachers and their schools, therefore needs to be reducing the balkanization between elementary and secondary schools through joint meetings, school visits, "buddy" systems between primary and high school students, shared science fairs, band days, cross appointments, gaining teaching experience across panels over the course of one's career and so on.

Balkanization creates stereotypes. Stereotypes reinforce fear and defensiveness. This is why we advocate linking within-school collegiality to wider networking among teachers as professionals.

## 8. Redefine Your Role to Include Responsibilities Outside the Classroom

Reform is systemic. Improvements inside the classroom depend on improvements outside it. The teacher of the 1990's must "take responsibility for more than the minimum, more than what goes on within the four walls of our classrooms" (Barth, 1990: 131). This means several things.

First, each teacher has an obligation to help increase the degree and quality of day-to-day interaction with other teachers. Even if done on a small scale regularly, this can make a very significant difference for other individual teachers, and for oneself.

Second, each teacher has a responsibility to try to understand and to attempt to improve the culture of the school. We have seen what collaborative cultures look like, and how much care and attention they require to

77

develop and to maintain (Chapter 3). Every teacher must be concerned about the health of the school as an organization. This does not mean getting obsessively involved in every aspect of school life, but it does mean taking some responsibility for the welfare of one's colleagues and the wider life of the school.

Third, every teacher is a leader. Depending on life and career circumstances, the leadership role at some stages will be significant—head of a curriculum committee, federation representative, mentor teacher, etc. At other times, it will be less formal — organizing the staff social, making materials available from a course you attended, helping colleagues use their computers etc. *All* teachers have a leadership contribution to make beyond their own classrooms, and should take action accordingly.

Fourth, redefining the teacher's role includes a responsibility to become knowledgeable about policy, and about professional and research issues in the wider provincial, national and international arenas. This does not mean having a second career as an academic. But it does mean connecting with the knowledge-base for improving teaching and schools. The more knowledgeable a teacher is about global educational and professional issues, the more resourceful he or she will be for students as well as for other teachers.

Finally, each and every teacher has a direct responsibility for helping to shape the quality of the next generation of teachers. Between 1988 and 1998 at least half the teaching population will be replaced. Fortunately, the calibre of new teachers in Ontario is very high. But, however good new teachers may be in academic qualifications and experiences, they still represent only raw potential. The conditions of teaching, especially at the beginning, influence and sometimes determine how good a new teacher will become. This *one* teacher will in turn affect the quality of learning experiences of hundreds of children over the next thirty years. What's worth fighting for is to make sure that these new teachers have better, much better, conditions for having a career. All teachers can make a contribution: offer to be a school associate, especially in innovative preservice programs; become a mentor in induction programs; support and praise other teachers who take on associate/mentor roles.

While these are specific forms of support, we must also emphasize that they proliferate when the entire staff of a school sees it as a whole-school responsibility to welcome and support newcomers. And when the whole culture of the school is routinely collaborative, the help that new teachers receive will not be seen as special or patronizing. It will be part of the helping culture that connects all teachers as learning professionals. Few things could be so important as interactive professionalism in the service of better beginnings for the thousands of new teachers currently entering the profession.

In short, classroom conditions will never improve until teachers take action to improve the conditions surrounding classrooms.

## 9.   Balance Work and Life

# Balancing the work and the life is an important protection against burnout. It also leads to more interesting teachers and more interesting teaching.

Wider involvements are important. Working with adults is as important as working with children. Teachers have responsibilities outside the classroom as well as within it. This means work, but not necessarily more work. Ideas and expertise gathered from colleagues can save work instead of making it. Priorities will also need to be set. Sometimes, a little reflective reading is a better choice than making three extra activity cards. Sometimes it may be better to let the children do the (less than perfect) bulletin board rather than do it all yourself (and use the time you save to work with a colleague).

Interactive professionalism requires time and support from administrators. But it also requires commitment and priority-setting from teachers. The worst scenario emerging from our guidelines would be one where teachers treated their commitment to collegiality as add-ons to all their existing work. It is important to avoid still further overload. (We are advocating interactive, not hyperactive professionalism). There are schools whose teachers regularly stay on until 7:00 p.m. and where their principals expect this. But these schools do not last long — neither do their teachers.

Particular projects and initiatives will require bursts of commitment and enthusiasm. But long hours, sustained over long periods will only lead to burn out. This is why priority-setting, sharing of responsibility, getting good ideas from colleagues etc. are important. The work is important, but so is the life. Teachers need to be watchful about establishing and maintaining a balance between them. Workaholics and careerists do not always make the best teachers.

In Chapter 2, we saw how women teachers often balance their work life with their family and personal life more effectively than many of their male colleagues. Another example of the importance of such a balance is the art teacher in Bennett's (1985) study of over 80 actual and intending art teachers. Bennett found that the majority had little interest in promotion or administration, in being department heads or principals, for instance. They were not at all "careerist" in the conventional sense. Their primary work and life satisfactions, rather, came from their art which gave them a parallel career, or another source of meaning and worth outside the school. This did not make them bad, cynical, or dissatisfied teachers, however. On the contrary their release from administration and career striving made them better, more fulfilled classroom teachers who could concentrate their energies on the quality and effectiveness of their classroom relationships with their students.

Avoidance of administration need not mean confinement to the classroom. There are other, more informal ways of getting involved with one's colleagues as we have seen. The art teachers' careers carry important lessons for other teachers. They point to the importance of developing interests, lives and selves outside school as well as in it. Think of your interests outside school. Do you cultivate these and bring them into your teaching? If you are a music teacher, do you play and perform? If you are a language arts specialists, do you read high quality literature or do personal writing? As a social studies teacher do you collect rock specimens or go on archaeological digs? When you take advanced qualifications, do you always take courses on how to *teach* better science and math, say, rather than rediscovering the mystery and wonder of science or mathematics themselves?

Balancing the work and the life is an important protection against burnout. It also leads to more interesting teachers and more interesting teaching.

## 10. Push and Support Principals and Other Administrators to Develop Interactive Professionalism

It is too much to expect that principals and vice-principals by themselves could transform the culture of the school. Interactive professionalism is enacted through hundreds of behaviours each week. No one or two people could possibly bear the burden of developing and maintaining strong collaborative cultures. Nor do we think that teachers should be in such a dependent position. This is why we see every teacher as a leader. Without widespread initiative and participation, total teachers and total schools simply will not develop.

The principal, however, is in a strategic position to help. There are several implications for teachers. First, teachers should have high expectations for their principals, vice-principals and other administrators to model interactive professionalism: to be knowledgeable about research and practice on teacher development; to set expectations and to facilitate teachers working together; to be kind, courteous and caring of colleagues and to give praise where it is due; to seek new ideas outside the school; and to want teachers to share their practices with colleagues in other schools and systems. Teachers, then, should push their principals to support collaboration by presenting ideas or otherwise sitting down with administrators to discuss what the school is and should be doing to promote teacher development.

Second, it is important that teachers not automatically accept apparent lack of interest on the part of an administrator at face value. Principals are total people too. As teaching is a lonely profession, the principalship is all the more so. Lack of time, overload of responsibilities, uncertainty about their roles in leading change, fear of appearing unknowledgeable, and the stress of attempting to balance professional and personal lives put the principal in a difficult position to meet expectations. Lack of attention may or may not mean lack of interest. Thus, teachers should test their assumptions more than once, and look for ways to involve the principal in supporting examples of teacher-teacher exchanges. While some principals may be reticent because of overload, or ambivalent about their new roles as change facilitators, our guess is that most principals would welcome positive initiatives coming from individuals and groups of teachers. After all, it helps them do, and be seen to be doing their job more effectively.

Third, when a new principal arrives, help to familiarize her or him with the existing culture, the way you do things around here, especially in relation to collaboration and making improvements. If a principal tries to drive through premature changes that are insensitive to the culture, gently provide feedback. The vice-principal may be able to help here. And if the principal continues, despite all your efforts, to be a lone wolf, uninvolved with the staff and hierarchical in her or his style of command, remember the principal will probably leave before you do! Have patience, and gear up for the next change and the opportunities it will bring.

Fourth, these days more and more vice-principals and principals are being appointed on the basis of their curricular and professional development leadership skills. In many school boards, it amounts to a new critical mass. It is crucial and timely that teachers be responsive to and supportive of these new leaders. If the latter are as good as they appear to be, they will not be looking for ways to impose their favourite programs. Rather, they will be seeking to work collaboratively with teachers to establish new cultures and practices of teaching. Teachers following the twelve guidelines in this section will contribute to major advances through working closely with principals who are themselves committed to teacher development.

In sum, teachers should look for multiple ways to push, support, respond to, and praise school administrators in working on continuous school improvement.

### 11. Commit to Continuous Improvement and Perpetual Learning

The single distinguishing characteristic of the best professionals in any field is that they consistently strive for better results, and are always learning to become more effective, from whatever source they can find. The teacher as career-long learner is central to our guidelines and to this booklet as a whole. As Block (1987) states it:

One of the fastest ways to get out of a bureaucratic cycle is to have as your goal to learn as much as you can about what you're doing. Learning and performance are intimately related; the high performers are those who learn most quickly (p. 86).

The message for the individual teacher is to demonstrate openness to learning and to contribute to other teachers' learning as a taken-for-granted habit of everyday life. Acquiring new skills, testing out practices, working with others on an improvement project, taking courses and workshops that are designed with follow up applications, and assessing and discussing results are among the many examples available.

Teachers should also be demanding of their schools and districts to provide learning opportunities and environments. Hart and Murphy (1990) compared high promise/ability teachers who had five or fewer years of teaching with average teachers with the same amount of experience. They found that the high group teachers assessed professional development opportunities in terms of how likely they were to have an impact on teaching and learning, and were more likely to get frustrated and think of career alternatives if the situation was not getting better. They were committed to making a difference, but only if the school was organized to do so. Our point is more radical. Teachers should push themselves to create the professional learning environments they want. It should be the worse, not the better teachers that resort to considering alternative careers.

## Teacher development and student development are reciprocally related.

## 12. Monitor and Strengthen the Connections Between Your Development and Students' Development

Throughout this monograph, and particularly in our discussion of reflective practice, we have repeatedly seen how teacher development and student development are closely intertwined. The value of teacher development and teacher collaboration must ultimately be judged by whether these changes make teachers better for their students in ways that teachers themselves can see. As Huberman (1990) puts it:

> Most teachers would derive more professional satisfaction from resuscitating 3 sullen, low-performing pupils on the brink of dropping out than on raising class-level achievement tests by half a standard deviation in 6 months (p. 29).

There is nothing wrong with improving achievement scores, but teachers working together and individually must see a difference in the involvement and progress of children.

The kind of professional growth of teachers we are talking about is intimately tied-up with making schools visibly better places for students. Some schools—facing the same problems and with the same resources—are better than other schools (Mortimore et al., 1988). One vital difference is that the better schools pay attention to and try to ascertain the quality of student experiences and progress using a wide range of measures. These more effective schools also have greater collegiality, but it is particularly valued because it explicitly focuses on greater student learning.

In effective schools, teachers working with other teachers and the administration, are preoccupied with "measuring what is important" (Peters, 1987). Simple, direct, meaningful, involved forms of monitoring become natural, regular concerns of all teachers.

In Chapter 3, we saw how commitment to risk and improvement created higher senses of "efficacy" among teachers, and with it, gains in student achievement. Student development prospered from teacher development. In Guideline 2, we saw how teachers can collect feedback from students much more systematically, through discussions, formative assessment and involvement in innovation, as well as through qualitative measures and formal reviews. In this respect, student development contributes to teacher development.

Teacher development and student development are reciprocally related. Schools that actively monitor and strengthen the relationship between teacher and student well-being and development will find that both benefit in mutually escalating ways.

## Guidelines for Principals

We have talked a lot in this monograph about the teacher's responsibility for improvement, for guarding what is good and supporting what is better. Because of their presence in the classroom, and because of their sheer numbers, teachers really are the key to change. There can be no improvement without the teacher. We have urged teachers to be responsive to change. We have urged them to make changes of their own. And we have urged them to proceed and persist with change in their wider school environment. The individual and collective efforts of teachers as supporters and initiators of improvement are vital. But where leadership and school environments are particularly and persistently unsupportive, the success of teacher efforts will be slim, short-lived or non-existent, and teachers will quickly learn not to make them. This is where the role of the principal is crucial.

In Chapter 2, we found that poor teachers are usually the products of poor schools. Schools, we noted, tend to get the teachers they deserve. Principals who control all the decisions, who obstruct initiative, who choose blame before praise, who see only problems where others see possibilities, are principals who create discouraged and dispirited teachers. It may not be ethically right for teachers to give up and withdraw in the face of such negativism or indifference from their leaders, but it is understandably human and the response that most teachers will adopt.

So the principal's role as a supporter and promoter of interactive professionalism is essential. This should involve helping teachers to understand their own situation in ways that provide insights and means of improving.

*What's Worth Fighting For In The Principalship?* contains a number of guidelines which we will not repeat here. We want to build on the ideas of this monograph instead. At the most basic level, the 12 teacher guidelines apply to principals in a double-barreled way. As a principal, you can substitute the word *principal* for *teacher* and apply the guidelines to yourself. Second, you can also use the guidelines as you work with teachers. The operative question is how can you stimulate and help teachers in your school to respond to and follow the twelve teacher guidelines.

Beyond this, we suggest eight guidelines to highlight the action needed. As before, they represent more of a mindset than a mandate. Individual principals should choose their own combination of actions that are appropriate to their own circumstances. The eight guidelines are:
1. Understand The Culture
2. Value Your Teachers: Promote Their Professional Growth

3. Extend What You Value
4. Express What You Value
5. Promote Collaboration; Not Cooptation
6. Make Menus, Not Mandates
7. Use Bureaucratic Means to Facilitate, Not to Constrain
8. Connect with the Wider Environment

**Short-term appointments, particularly common where vice-principals are concerned, can place leaders under even greater pressure to make quick changes and demonstrate visible leadership qualities in a way that offers little opportunity to understand and appreciate the existing school culture.**

## 1. Understand Your School's Culture

For better or worse, culture is a powerful force. As Deal and Peterson (1987:12) say, "trying to shape it, change it, or fight it can have serious repercussions". They cite several examples of well intentioned mistakes, including the following:

Shortly after a principal arrived, he decided that a celebration of the school's "best" teachers would illustrate what the school should value and provide properly recognized role models for other teachers to emulate. On the appointed day, the principal waited alone in a room full of refreshments and decorated with banners. All the teachers had boycotted the event. His celebration had backfired because it violated the values and traditions of the school.

Deal and Peterson suggest that principals begin by asking "What is the culture of the school, its values, traditions, assumptions, beliefs and ways?"

Many principals in new positions, fired by the enthusiasm of leadership and their visions for the future, can be *too* eager to initiate change. Some principals do so out of insensitivity, failing to appreciate that even small changes can transgress sacred elements of the school culture. Connelly and Clandinin (1988), for instance, note how well-meant themes and projects proposed by the principal can interfere with long-standing and strongly valued seasonal rhythms and rituals like Halloween or Christmas to which teachers are deeply attached and committed. Other principals initiate quick and early change with a more bullish, or even bullying intent. They may even feel they are acting on a superintendent's mandate to "turn the school around". Short-term appointments, particularly common where vice-principals are concerned, can place leaders under even greater pressure to make quick changes and demonstrate visible leadership qualities in a way that offers little opportunity to understand and appreciate the existing school culture.

Our first guideline, then, is simple to state, but not easy to follow. *Understand the school and its culture before changing it!* Put priority on meaning before management. Take time. Be patient. Hold back on premature disapproval before you are in a position to judge fairly. Tradition is as important as change (Louden, 1991). Effective improvement means more than change. It also involves conserving what is good. Shrewd conservation requires deep understanding. Understanding the culture is not just a passive process. Nias and her colleagues (1989) argue that awareness is at the heart of it. Such awareness can and should be highly active. It involves lots of observation, getting out of the office, walking around the school or what Peters (1987) call *Management By Walking About*. Active awareness also involves high amounts of listening and talking to determine what teachers are doing, what they value, what are their satisfactions and dissatisfactions, their sources of pride and concern. Deal and Peterson suggest that when "reading the culture", principals should ask questions like: "Who is most influential?" "What do people say when asked what the school stands for?", "What do people wish for; what are their unfulfilled goals or dreams?"

Active awareness and understanding is vital to being an effective leader within the culture of the school. In addition, it provides routine opportunities for principals to express what they value, what they can contribute to the culture, without imposing their views as threatening edicts. This brings us to our next guideline.

# Appreciating the teacher as a total person and not just as a bundle of competencies or deficits is central to this guideline.

### 2. Value Your Teachers: Promote Their Professional Growth

In Chapter 2, we saw, through the work of Huberman and others, how easy and common it is for experienced teachers to get discarded and disvalued by their principals and colleagues. When such teachers are made to feel they are not part of things, when their wisdom and expertise are not sought or valued, and when their teaching styles and strategies are dismissively viewed as out-of-date and no longer valid, they understandably become disenchanted and resistant to change. When a school has one or two bad teachers, this is usually a problem with the individual teachers. When it has many bad teachers, it is a problem of leadership.

A real challenge for the principal is to find something to value in all the school's teachers. Even poor or mediocre teachers have good points that can present opportunities to give praise and raise self-esteem. Good elementary teachers do this with their students, and principals should do likewise with their teachers. Appreciating the teacher as a total person and not just as a bundle of competencies or deficits is central to this guideline. To develop this appreciation, active awareness, observation and communication are central. To value the teacher, one must know the teacher in order to find things to value.

This kind of knowledge, acquired informally through observation and conversation, and more formally through evaluation and supervision, can provide a springboard to professional growth. Knowing the teacher helps in identifying what the teacher's needs might be and what kinds of support, experiences and opportunities will be appropriate. The worst thing to do is to write off apparently poor or mediocre teachers as dead wood, and seek easy administrative solutions in transfers or retirements. Once they are marginalized, it is not difficult to shut these teachers out altogether. Try doing the hard thing, the right thing, the ethical thing, and explore ways of bringing these teachers back in instead.

## When a school has one or two bad teachers, this is usually a problem with the individual teacher. When it has many bad teachers, it is a problem of leadership.

### 3. Extend What You Value

In Chapter 2, we argued that valuing teachers involves more than generosity of spirit. It requires breadth of educational vision too. Narrow goals, or singular commitments to specific programs like whole language or manipulative math, are exclusive rather than inclusive in their impact. If principals demand complete conversion to learning centres, for instance, those committed to and experienced in other approaches will be made to feel incompetent and devalued as a result. Recognizing that many other long-standing alternatives are not valueless, acknowledging their appropriateness for some settings, and supporting their combination and integration with new strategies will be more likely to keep experienced teachers involved and included in improvement. Partisan commitments to particular approaches will not.

Extending what you value is important if you are to recognize the genuine worth of your staff. But this does not mean valuing anything or having no values at all. Unjustifiable practice should not be allowed to persist. Teaching that consistently hurts children, or fails to make improvements, is indefensible. At the same time, failure to comply wholeheartedly with preferred programs like cooperative learning should not be criticized so readily. Research on instructional strategies supports this view. A wide repertoire of strategies, applied flexibly and sensitively, is more effective than commitment to any particular approach (Hargreaves and Earl, 1991). Valuing teachers who constantly seek to expand their repertoires and who search for opportunities to learn from their colleagues is more productive than endorsing a particular program or method. This kind of valuing is broad, but it is definite, and it is one that will promote inclusive commitment to, rather than exclusive rejection of, your teachers.

Extending what you value is one of the most important moves you can make in promoting the professional development of all your teachers, rather than the advancement of a chosen, innovative few.

## 4. Express What You Value

We have said it is important to value your teachers and to know them well enough to do that. We have also stressed the importance of extending what you value so that praise and recognition are not unduly scarce and so that teachers can show their worth in different ways. What is also important is communicating and demonstrating what you value, expressing yourself through your leadership.

This is best done not through preemptive statements of policy and purpose, although this can be an important input as the school develops its mission together (as we shall see in Guideline 7). Particularly in the early stages of a principalship, though, communicating and demonstrating what you value is best done through behaviour and example, through what you *do* and what you *are* on a day-to-day basis. This is appropriate even when you are learning the school's culture, so that teachers can gradually develop a sense of what is important for you, what is at the core of your values. Demonstrating what you value remains important even as you strengthen the culture or change it with your staff. This process of cultural formation and reformation should be democratic, as we shall see, but you are the school's designated leader and you should show what it is you have to contribute. Principals should certainly beware of squeezing schools into their own personal visions, but they should not hide their lights under a bushel basket either.

What kinds of behaviour and example best demonstrate one's values as a principal? Deal and Kennedy (1982) advocate reinforcing and developing the core values and norms of the school through modeling, coaching and attention; through the design of ceremonies, rituals and traditions; through the recounting of stories, along with the anointing of heroes and heroines; and through use of the informal network.

Nias et al. (1989) and Leithwood and Jantzi (1990) also advise using symbols and rituals to express cultural values. This is especially important where what is being valued is collaborative work and perpetual learning. Behaviour that is helpful here includes celebrating staff and student contributions to achievement, in public presentations and staff meetings; writing private notes to staff to express thanks for special efforts; encouraging and supporting teachers to share experiences with each other; participating in informal celebrations; revealing something of one's private self as a person; asking for help where appropriate; and showing that one is vulnerable, not invincible.

In short, the principal as collaborative symbol is one of the basic keys to forming and reforming the school culture. What he or she does, pays attention to, appreciates and talks or writes about all count. All this requires work, effort, and vigilance. But what we are recommending cannot be reduced to a list of strategies and techniques that can be learned and applied in a straightforward way. Rather, we are speaking of behaviour that expresses core values. While it does take effort to do the things we have described, the important thing is to be authentic. The heart matters as much as the head. If the heart is preoccupied with tight control, no amount of headwork, of learned behaviours and techniques, will counteract it. It will merely make you more manipulative, not more sharing. In expressing what you value, you too, therefore, like your teachers, must listen to your inner voice and address the sincerity of what you are attempting. Otherwise, your supposedly symbolic behaviours will ultimately be exposed as hollow and contrived, which brings us to our next guideline.

# Principals have no monopoly on wisdom.

### 5. Promote Collaboration, Not Cooptation

The principal has a crucial role to play in shaping and developing the culture of the school. We have already discussed the importance of the principal's own behaviour in modeling what is valued. There is a body of literature, currently popular, which presents the leader as shaper of the culture and which outlines specific strategies for carrying out that role. However, we want to question some aspects of that literature. We believe it is too accepting of current norms of what constitutes the principalship; norms which, despite concessions to sharing and involvement, still construe the principalship in fundamentally hierarchical terms.

Our main disagreement is with the place of vision in the development of school culture. We do not dispute the importance of vision, of shared purpose, and of direction among a school's staff. Nor do we dispute that visions sometimes need to be clarified or changed. The crucial question, though, is "Whose vision is this?" For some writers, the principal's role in helping develop school culture becomes one of manipulating the culture and its teachers to conform to the principal's own vision. Deal and Peterson (1987: 14), for example, urge that once principals have come to understand their school's culture, they should then ask, "If it matches my conception of a 'good school', what can I do to reinforce or strengthen existing patterns? If my vision is at odds with the existing mindset, values or ways of acting, what can be done to change or shape the culture?" For Deal and Peterson, this is part of the solution to the challenge of school leadership. For us, it is part of the problem.

"My vision", "my teachers", "my school" are proprietary claims and attitudes which suggest an ownership of the school which is personal rather than collective, imposed rather than earned, and hierarchical rather than democratic. With *visions* as singular as this, teachers soon learn to suppress their *voice*. It does not get articulated. Management becomes manipulation. Collaboration become cooptation. Worst of all, having teachers conform to the principal's vision minimizes the possibilities for principal learning. It reduces the opportunities for principals to learn that parts of their own vision may be flawed, and that some teachers' visions may be as valid or more valid than theirs. Vision-building is a two-way street where principals learn from as much as they contribute to others (Bolman and Deal 1990, Louis and Miles 1990).

This does not mean that principals' visions are unimportant. The quality and clarity of their visions may have helped mark them for leadership. Principals have no monopoly on wisdom. Nor should they be immune from the questioning, inquiry and deep reflection in which we have asked teachers to engage. Principals' visions should therefore be provisional and open to change. They should be part of the collaborative mix. The authority of principals' views should not be presumed because of whose views they are, but because of their quality and richness.

Ultimately — and we have said this throughout — the responsibility for vision-building is a collective, not an individual one. Collaboration should mean creating the vision together, not complying with the principal's own. All stake-holders should be involved in illuminating the mission and purposes of the school. The articulation of different voices may create initial conflict, but this should be confronted and worked through. It is part of the collaborative process.

Sharing leadership and promoting professional development is deeper and more complex than is often assumed. Shared leadership is not just involvement in a school decision-making committee, nor is it having teachers participate in all decisions. Professional development is not simply a matter of encouraging teachers to become involved in a variety of inservice activities. Centrally, shared leadership and access to resources are closely related. Opportunity for leadership opportunities without resources is stultifying. Availability of resources, especially human collaborative ones, stimulates initiative-taking and leadership. All studies linking principal behaviour to school improvement have found this to be the case.

Louis and Miles (1990: 232-6) suggest five "strategies for involvement":

- Power sharing
- Rewards for staff
- Openness, inclusiveness
- Expanding leadership roles
- Patience

The principal has to be willing to share control, show vulnerability, and look for ways to involve the reticent or the opposed (the openness, inclusiveness theme) rather than just the favourite few. If the whole school culture is to change, it will be necessary to spread responsibility for leadership beyond heads of divisions, for example. Taking into account the total person, effective principals know that leadership can take many different forms and levels of magnitude. When the right connections are made, the release of energy can be powerful. As Barth (1990) says, "the moment of greatest learning for any of us is when we find ourselves responsible for a problem that we care desperately to resolve" (p. 136). The message is stimulate, look for, and celebrate examples of teacher leadership.

The effective principal all the while fosters collaboration. Mortimore and his colleagues (1988) found that the involvement of the deputy head or vice principal (as well as staff) in decision-making was a characteristic of the more effective schools in their sample. The principal is a role model of collaboration inside and outside the school. Interestingly and ironically, principals who share authority and establish conditions conducive to empowerment, actually *increase* their influence over what is accomplished in the school, as they work with staff to bring about improvement.

Teacher development and teacher learning have been pervasive themes in this monograph. Thus, the principal who is a micropolitical animal within the board, who works actively on acquiring resources and opportunities related to teacher learning or professional development can contribute enormously to collaborative cultures (Smith and Andrews, 1989). Sometimes this means money, equipment or materials, but it also involves time, access to other ideas and practices, and opportunity to receive and give assistance. As Louis and Miles stress, acquiring content-related resources (equipment, materials) requires *additional* resources (time, assistance) for effective utilization (p. 260).

We want to emphasize again that each guideline should not be taken literally or in isolation. It is the mind-set about the totality of guidelines that counts. In this case, for example, it is not a "catch and grab" quantitative expansion of resources and learning opportunities that is needed. In addition to brand-new resources, principals and staff can also "rework" existing resources (like altering the timetable to enable teachers to get together). Success begets success. Generating new resources creates opportunities to acquire even more.

Selectivity about certain kinds of professional development is also important in order to avoid contrived collegiality and other desultory professional development experiences. Mortimore et al. (1988) found that schools were *less* effective in those cases where principals encouraged and permitted teachers to attend an indiscriminate array of in-service workshops and courses. By contrast, in schools where teachers were encouraged to participate in selective in-service programs, "for good reason", there was a positive impact on pupil progress and teacher development (p. 224).

In sum, shared leadership does not mean handing over the reins of power and opting out. But it does not mean using collaboration to steer through one's own personal views either. As leader among leaders, or first among equals, the principal should be engaged in promoting involvement and learning in as many parts of the school as possible. The principal too is an *interactive* professional, and learns as well as leads through collaboration.

If there is one justifiable vision that is generic to our argument, it is a vision of particular ways of working together and of commitment to perpetual learning and improvement. Substantive visions of whole language, active learning or academic emphasis are contestable visions over which the principal should have no special prerogative and which should be decided collaboratively, as a staff. But process visions about how schools work together are central to continuing improvement. Such visions about collaboration, helping, perpetual learning, risk-taking, trust in processes, and the like are central to our case. It is legitimate, indeed essential, that principals have such generic visions, that they occupy their heart as well as their head, and that they are fulfilled through their actions as well as their words. This real and not cosmetic commitment to collaborative working and shared leadership is fundamentally worth fighting for.

**Collaboration should mean creating the vision together, not complying with the principal's own ... The articulation of different voices may create initial conflict, but this should be confronted and worked through. It is part of the collaborative process.**

### 6.   Make Menus, Not Mandates

Even the commitment to collaboration needs to be exercised flexibly and responsibly, though. In Chapter 3, we catalogued the many different forms that collaboration can take. For administrators, while teacher collaboration holds great promise, it also contains perils. Drawing on our earlier discussions of contrived collegiality, we will highlight two of these.

First, is the peril of assuming that collaboration takes one form, thereby pressuring teachers to adopt it. Mandatory peer coaching, compulsory team teaching, required collaborative planning—measures as inflexible and insensitive as these are to be avoided. They fail to recognize the diverse forms that collaborative work can take. They prescribe narrow techniques that may not suit some people or contexts, and make people lose sight of the broader collaborative principle which gave rise to them and which could command wider support. They therefore offend the discretionary judgement of teachers that is at the core of interactive professionalism. Mandating specific kinds of collaboration is not empowering but disempowering.

We therefore advocate putting menus before mandates. Don't force through one particular approach. Develop awareness of, commitment to, and experience in the general collaborative principle. Document, show examples of, and perhaps give workshops across the array of collaborative practices that is available. Commit to the principle, but empower teachers to select from the wide range of practices the ones that suit them best. Continue to foster shared experiences and perpetual learning, so that knowledge and experience of these different practices grow over time.

Commitment to collaboration is important. But there is a second peril to beware of here. We have frequently stressed the necessity of maintaining a precarious balance between collaboration and individuality. We have said that individuality and solitude should be a high priority for teachers. What principals do can also have powerful consequences for teacher individuality. While commitment to collaboration is important, over-commitment or compulsion can be damaging. Increasing the commitment to collaborative work and having most teachers try some aspect of it is essential. But working for a 100 percent adoption rate is unrealistic and undesirable. Appreciating the total teacher means recognizing that most teachers will plan or teach some things better alone than together. The solitary mode has its place. Group think has its dangers.

There will also be some teachers who, despite every encouragement, still want to work alone. Where such teachers are weak or incompetent, refusal to work with and learn from others might legitimately be seen as part of a case for disciplinary action or dismissal. But not all individualistic teachers are weak teachers. A few are strong, even excellent classroom practitioners. They may be eccentric, Prima Donna-ish, difficult to work with as colleagues, but skilled in their own classrooms, nonetheless. Where, after every encouragement, such teachers still insist on being loners, they should be allowed to do so. Their idiosyncratic excellence should not be punished in pursuit of the collegial norm. You will only make them worse teachers if you do.

So commitment to collaboration is worth fighting for, but not with administrative and ideological inflexibility. Above all else, even above collaboration, respect for teacher discretion is paramount, providing this does no harm to students. This is why menus should prevail over mandates.

## 7. Use Bureaucratic Measures To Facilitate, Not To Constrain

Bureaucracy is often seen as an obstacle to change: "You can't do it because of the timetable!" "The Board won't allow it!" "The parents will object!" These are the binds that bureaucracy can put on our improvement efforts, if we let it! Bureaucracy can also be a problem if we convert sound principles of collaboration and improvement into inflexible systems of bureaucratic control. Much of the success of Teachers' Centres, for instance, collapsed once they were taken out the the hands of teachers themselves and run by school board bureaucracies instead. This is the problem of contrived collegiality, of bureaucracy as constraint.

But bureaucratic means are not necessarily evil. They can also be used to facilitate and support our improvement efforts. They can be placed in the service of collaborative cultures, to help institutionalize new organizational structures favourable to continuous improvement. Principals have a number of administrative means already at their disposal. Many fail to incorporate them into an overall strategy. The most effective collaborative principals utilize and build on existing bureaucratic procedures.

The following five mechanisms are among those used by such principals:

• Public endorsements and official policy
• School organization, planning, and scheduling
• Decision-making structures
• Staffing procedures
• Evaluation

To start with official policy, Little (1987) observes that "principals and others in positions of influence promote collegiality by declaring that they value team efforts and by describing in some detail what they think that means" (p. 508). This is partly related to symbolic leadership (Guideline 1), but shows up here in the form of policy statements—widely endorsed by staff—which explicitly state that working together for teacher and student development is of the highest priority. These policies reflect and reiterate "what we stand for", and "the way we work around here".

The organization of the school provides many opportunities for inhibiting or expanding collaboration. Research on collaborative school cultures reports that principals effective in developing and maintaining such cultures use planning and scheduling directly for that purpose (Hargreaves and Wignall, 1989; Hargreaves, forthcoming; Leithwood and Jantzi, 1990). They do this by providing time for collaborative planning during the workday, timetabling students to allow teachers to work together, and keeping school improvement on the forefront of meeting agendas. Giving one's own time by covering teachers' classes, using preparation time to increase teacher-teacher contact, facilitating common planning times and regularly scheduled curriculum meetings, and finding imaginative ways for altering the timetable to support cooperative work are all constructive examples of altering the organization of the school to suit collaborative ends.

In some cases, where existing structures make opportunities for collaboration almost impossible, solutions may need to be quite radical. One example of this at the secondary level is the proposed abolition of subject divisions and subject departments in Grade 9 in order to establish smaller core groups of teachers who work together with students across integrated units of study. One objective of this restructuring is to increase cross-subject collegiality and reduce departmental balkanization among secondary school teachers (Hargreaves and Earl, 1990). Another example of productive restructuring is the establishment of new roles such as peer coaches, mentor teachers, resource teachers, curriculum leaders, division heads and so on.

Decision-making structures and procedures, especially those related to collaboration and continuous improvement, can also be used to advantage. School improvement teams are one example of this. If the school is required by the district to develop a school improvement or school growth plan — as most are — why not use it as an opportunity to work through the teacher and principal guidelines described in this monograph.

The recruitment and selection of staff can be another powerful strategy. Leithwood and Jantzi (1990) note that effective principals in their sample used staffing procedures to effect improvement by "selecting new staff based on improvement priorities and willingness to collaborate, involving staff in hiring decisions" (p. 25). However, we expressly want to emphasize that just as teachers need to take responsibility beyond their classrooms, principals must also take responsibility beyond their own schools. Aggressively recruiting the best teachers from other schools while transferring the least effective to whomever will take them is ultimately self defeating — in two ways.

First, what goes around, comes around! Eventually, you too will have to take your turn in receiving teachers discarded by other schools. Aggressive selection will only yield temporary success, therefore. Second, while aggressive selection may create collaborative schools, it will not create collaborative systems. Schools that select aggressively and have unusual powers to hire and fire become innovative exceptions. Infuriatingly, they are then often held up by their systems as beacons of improvement which the rest, creamed of their best teachers, are expected to, but are frustratingly unable to follow.

Individually and together, principals have a responsibility to help upgrade the learning opportunities for all teachers in the system. Acting in narrowly competitive ways, prematurely giving up on some of one's own staff, and investing too much in the selection of the fittest, produce short term advantages at best — and even then, only for a minority of schools, not for systems as a whole.

Finally, evaluation procedures can also be used to foster teacher development. Performance appraisal schemes that are growth-based can be used to make collaboration and commitment to improvement valued and assessed activities. We caution, as before, that many routes should be made available for achieving these ends, according to teacher goals and circumstances. But if there is to be evaluation, you should evaluate what you most value. Collaboration, commitment to continuous improvement, risk-taking, breadth and flexibility in instruction, and articulation of voice should therefore be among these. Student achievement and performance data, widely defined and interpreted, should also be used as a springboard for action, provided that the other guidelines are followed. Effective collaborative schools are actively interested in how well they are doing, and seek evaluative data to monitor and improve on progress.

## 8.   Connect With the Wider Environment

Schools do not thrive unless they are actively plugged into their environments, contributing to and responding to the issues of the day. This means two things for the principal. First, he or she needs to be involved outside the school, especially in learning activities. Some examples include: participating in peer coaching projects among principals; working with other principals and administrators in the board to improve professional development for principals; visiting other schools outside as well as inside one's board; spending time in the community; finding out about the latest practices as reported in the professional literature and disseminating ideas about one's own school practices through speeches, workshops and/or writing. It will be necessary to be selective, but ongoing involvement outside the school, in some form, is essential for perpetual learning and effectiveness.

Second, principals should help the school deal with the wider environment. Sometimes this will involve contending with the overload of unwanted or unreasonable change. It might involve urging and facilitating a move toward school-based decision-making within the board. Mostly, however, we suggest that the highest priority be placed by the principal on helping teachers widen the contacts with the professional world outside school. Contacts should be made not just with schools doing similar things, but also with schools involved in different activities, even opposites. Contrast is an important prompt for critical self-reflection. Going "outside the frame" beyond one's normal traditions, is a great source of learning and improvement.

Principals can do a variety of things to help broaden the horizons and contacts of teachers. Encouraging and supporting teachers to link up with other teachers within the district would be one example. Forming an association with a local faculty of education is another. Encouraging participation in professional development activities of a teacher's federation is a third. Increasingly, more and more formal networks, collaborations and coalitions are being formed that involve partnerships across institutions for fixed periods of time (Fullan, Bennett and Rolheiser-Bennett, 1990). Alliances also provide power bases of support for moving in desired directions (Block, 1987).

The gist of this last guideline is that collaborative schools will not retain their vitality or longevity unless they are part of a larger movement. Lieberman and Miller (1990) rightly observe that "teachers who see themselves as part of a school in the process of change must also see themselves as part of a profession in the process of change" (p. 117).

## Guidelines for School Systems

# They transfer principals between schools as if they are trading baseball cards.

This booklet is for teachers and principals and is based on the premise that they must push outward to achieve the improvements they want. Therefore, our advice for school systems is not elaborate. It is provocative, however. The most general advice, of course, is that school systems should take action to encourage, support and propel schools to internalize the guidelines and the spirit of reform presented on the previous pages.

This, in itself, is not controversial. But the specific implications are and we want to spell these out. As Sarason (1990) argues, the failure of educational reform has been persistent and predictable — for two reasons. First, it has failed because we have tinkered with innovations one at a time. Much of the rest of the system has been left untouched and has systematically undermined our reform efforts every time we have made them. We need to tackle different parts of the problem simultaneously, to see their connectedness, and to appreciate and act on the big picture. School systems, from Boards to Ministries, are better placed than anyone else to do this. They can help foster and facilitate real senses of vision and connectedness, system-wide.

Second, reform has failed because teachers are not good at sharing power with students, principals are not good at sharing power with teachers, and school systems are not good at sharing power with their schools. Power is a major problem at every level. There is growing evidence that not just individual schools, but entire school systems possess distinctive organizational cultures (Coleman & LaRocque, 1990, Leithwood et al., 1990, Rosenholtz, 1989). The culture of the district impacts on and helps shape the culture of its schools. Consequently, school districts can hardly expect principals to empower their teachers if they do not in turn empower their principals as well as their teachers. Some systems still act as if principals and teachers can be dragooned into being democratic, or compelled to be cooperative! They transfer principals between schools as if they are baseball cards. If school systems are to create total teachers and total schools, they need to grasp the realities of empowerment, not just the rhetoric.

These two principles of *connectedness* and of real, not cosmetic *empowerment* underpin our guidelines for school boards — guidelines which will build the capacity of teachers and schools to take the innumerable daily actions necessary to make a difference. Our four guidelines are:

1. Develop more trust and risk as a system: especially in selection, promotion and development processes
2. Foster increased interaction and empowerment in the system
3. Give curriculum content back to the schools
4. Restructure your administration to meet current needs

## 1. Trust, Risk and Selection

Rosenholtz (1989) found that not only schools, but school districts in her sample were "moving", while others were "stuck". The districts on the move had a much higher proportion of schools that were moving or learning-enriched for both teachers and students. One of the major distinguishing characteristics between the two sets of districts was that the effective ones placed a great deal of emphasis on selection criteria and procedures, and on learning opportunities, once staff were selected.

In operational terms, boards (as many now do) need to establish explicit selection criteria which make it crystal clear they are looking for people who can demonstrate initiative-taking, curriculum leadership, and a commitment to interactive forms of professional development. They need to back this up with strong expectations and plenty of opportunity to participate in the latest learning practices. They also need to address all parts of the teacher education continuum, through involvement in pre-service teacher education experiments, careful selection and induction programs for new teachers, mentoring and peer opportunities for all teachers, short and long range leadership development programs for teachers and administrators and so forth.

Effective systems require special kinds of trust and risk, of the sort we applied to teachers. And these need to be central to selection, promotion and professional development procedures. Earlier, we saw that trust and risk are reciprocally connected. In smaller, more stable organizations, collaboration mainly depends on trust in individuals. This kind of trust minimizes risk. In more complex and rapidly changing organizations, we saw that another kind of trust is also needed — trust in expertise and in processes of collaboration and continuous improvement. This kind of trust maximizes the benefits of risk.

If school systems really are serious about promoting these second kinds of trust and risk, they must incorporate them into their own administrative cultures. There are very specific implications for promotion procedures here. In many boards, promotion to and within administrative positions mainly depends on trust in individuals. It can ensure that new principals and other administrators will be attuned to the system culture. It can also provide means of rewarding excellence in the system. But promotion solely according to trust in individuals can also perpetuate patronage with its "old boy" and "new girl" networks. It can create dependency and conformity among those keen for promotion. It can reduce risk.

As complex and rapidly changing organizations, school systems themselves must be more risk-oriented, trusting in processes as well as people. They should increase their opportunities for learning by actively recruiting diverse expertise from other systems. Their promotional policies should be outward as well as inward looking. We therefore recommend that school systems commit to making outside as well as inside promotional appointments. This will demonstrate their willingness to place the priorities of risk over priorities of control. For some boards, this will be a difficult transition to make. And as they break out of what are, in some cases, rather monopolistic promotional procedures, they will need strong support from their federations. Together, this commitment to greater system risk is worth fighting for.

## 2. School-System Interaction and Empowerment

**While individual schools can become highly collaborative without the board, they cannot stay collaborative in the absence of active board support.**

The school is the "unit of change", but this concept is frequently misunderstood. Sirotnik (1987) suggests that the school should be conceptualized as the *centre* of change. "To say something is at the centre implies a good deal around it" (p. 21). And:

We are led to the organization, eg., the school as the centre of change. We are not lead naively to see the school as isolated from its sociopolitical context, able to engage in miraculous self-renewing activities without district, community, state, and federal support (p. 25).

There is increasing evidence that the most effective schools are in boards in which there is close ongoing *interaction* between school and board staff (Coleman and La Rocque, 1990, Fullan, 1991). Discussion and negotiation of school improvement plans, access to resources, gathering and reviewing performance data of importance to the school and examining staffing and inservice needs are all evident in these productive relationships. Of course, the interaction must focus on the right things, and be developmentally-oriented according to the guidelines outlined earlier for teachers and principals. But it should be stressed that while individual schools can become highly collaborative without the board, they cannot *stay* collaborative in the absence of active board support.

That support requires empowerment for schools to take more initiative than many now do, and to do so within very broad system guidelines and priorities. Moves to school-based management are encouraging these kinds of changes. Procedures for allocating principals to schools should also work to support rather than ignore these developments. In some systems, principals are rotated too frequently and allocated to new positions with little warning or consultation. These procedures need to be reviewed. Otherwise, disempowered principals merely create disempowered staffs. What school boards want principals to do, they should do themselves. Positive interaction needs empowerment. Empowerment means taking more risks and relinquishing tight control. Are school boards up to this challenge? Principals and teachers should pressure them to face and overcome it.

## 3. Give Curriculum Back To The Schools

Meaningful collaboration requires having substantial and ongoing things to collaborate about. This means that teachers and principals must be given more control over curriculum and instruction. Dumping curriculum packages on teachers, however sophisticated and worthwhile they might be, ultimately tends to make teachers deskilled and dependent (Apple and Jungck, 1991). As a result, with each new package and set of guidelines, many teachers replay the iniquities of innovation. They simplify it, ignore it, misinterpret it, slow it down, or imagine they are already doing it. When excessive amounts of content are externally prescribed, be this at board or Ministerial level, teachers become preoccupied with coverage. They concentrate on the compulsory core at the expense of the interesting options, take less risks with time-consuming inquiry methods, and so on. These problems seem to become particularly acute from Grades 7 and on, when content demands get especially heavy (Hargreaves and Earl, 1990).

The rhetoric of school reform and of system goals is one which often extols the virtues of skills, attitudes, concepts and problem-solving. The reality elevates content as the prime requirement. Externally devised content has become constraining rather than enabling. It has created dependency in teachers, overload on schools and wastefulness of administrative energy. We therefore propose giving most of the responsibility for curriculum content back to schools. This will create something substantial for teachers to collaborate about. The shared responsibilities for and opportunities to develop content, we believe, will unleash energy and enthusiasm among teachers as they are able to capitalize freely on their collective strengths and expertise as they improve learning for their students.

This does not mean developing curriculum from scratch or in isolation. Board priorities will remain important, but the balance needs to be redefined. The following measures (outlined more fully in Hargreaves, 1989) may help with achieving such a redefinition.

- As a board (or Ministry), set down broad guidelines with your teachers in each subject or curriculum area, in terms of skills, concepts and attitudes, and perhaps some information. Ensure they reflect broader educational goals.
- Make it each school's ultimate responsibility to select or develop contents through which the skills, concepts and attitudes will be realized.
- So that teachers do not have to invent everything anew or all at once, and so that you know where best to concentrate your resources as a board, produce a limited number of sample contents for each area of learning. There should always be more than one set of contents for each area, so that teachers avoid dependency and retain opportunity to exercise discretion.

- Use school board consultants to work with schools in helping them develop their contents, and in validating those contents as meeting board guidelines.
- Develop an information and resource network so that schools can share the contents they have developed with each other.

A shift of this kind will mean profound changes of role for many consultants. Recent research by Ross and Regan (1989) on school board consultants indicates that inexperienced ones tend to work with teachers and build from their concerns, whereas experienced ones put more emphasis on implementing board priorities. Ross and Regan attribute this difference to growth in expertise. We see it more as a case of creeping so-cialization into board priorities and procedures. The role of the consultant is currently under review in a number of school systems. For too long, consultants have spent disproportionate amounts of time on one-shot workshops, in board administration, and on curriculum guideline writing teams. More time needs to be spent developing ongoing relationships and support for particular groups of schools they get to know exceptionally well.

Giving curriculum content back to schools is a big step for schools and a bigger one for their boards. It is a serious test of the commitment to empowerment on everyone's part. Without that commitment, most sys-tem-wide collaboration will eventually weaken and collapse. This sce-nario of giving curriculum back to the schools is not far fetched. Michelle Landsberg's (1990) commissioned report for the Toronto Teachers' Fed-eration is a case in point. She stresses:

> Only when parents feel that their particular children's needs are being met, and when teachers are free to work together in forging a style and curriculum appropriate to their students, do schools enjoy the autonomy and popular support which are essential to their suc-cess. The task of the provincial ministry and local boards is to set province-wide goals and standards and to provide the funds, re-search, the resource materials and the means to achieve those goals (p. 6).

**We therefore suggest that at all levels — from the board administration to the school professional development — a good proportion of staff development resources be allocated not to workshops and inservices, but to opportunities**

# for teachers to learn from, observe and network with each other.

## 4. Restructure The Administration

Our last guideline is quite brief because it is implied so strongly in the other three. We recommend that systems review their administrative structures and reorganize them if necessary so they can meet their broad objectives of connectedness and empowerment effectively.

One of the greatest impediments to achieving these objectives is the balkanization of administrative structures in many school boards, particularly between program and staff development sections. This often leads to program departments developing new materials and approaches, and staff development being made responsible for implementing them. Or it means staff development having to foster teacher development or collaborative cultures in ways that do not infringe on the territorial claims of the program department. As management and curriculum development become more school-based, this kind of split will prove particularly unhelpful. Curriculum development and teacher development are inseparable (Hargreaves, 1989). Their balkanization into different departments will simply keep them apart, confining staff development to innocuous or short-lived initiatives. Combining and restructuring administrative responsibilities right up to superintendent level, across program and staff development seems to us an important priority for supporting the other guidelines in this text.

We have also considered ways in which consultants might be deployed more effectively with small groups of schools on a continuing basis, rather than across the system in ways that relate to their subjects. Some systems are already moving in this direction to give more continuing on-site support to their schools.

A third recommendation concerns staff development budgets and priorities. In an extensive analysis of district-level staff development budgets, Little (1990) has found that the vast majority of those budgets are allocated to trainers and administrators, not to teachers themselves. And yet we have seen that one of the most effective forms of teacher development is where teachers learn from each other. We therefore suggest that at all levels — from the board administration to the school professional development committee — a good proportion of staff development resources be allocated not to workshops and inservices, but to opportunities for teachers to learn from, observe, and network with each other. Supply coverage and travel expenses, so that teachers can visit other classes and work alongside other teachers inside and outside their own schools, are legitimate uses of staff development resources. They may not be as glitzy or high status as other uses, but on a cumulative basis, they can be highly effective.

In summary, redefining the relationship between program and staff development sections, reconstructing the role of consultants, and reallocating much of the staff development budget from trainers to teachers are changes worth fighting for at the system level.

# It is essential that those outside the school come to recognize the power of developing total teachers and total schools.

## Conclusion

We have not examined other vital aspects of school-based futures. In particular, what's worth fighting for, for parents and for students, has not been spelled out. This might well be the subject for a future booklet. Rather, we focused on teachers in particular, because they are the key to unlocking the future for parents and students, and because they have been neglected and misunderstood in attempts at school reform.

It is essential that those outside the school come to recognize the power of developing total teachers and total schools. But individual teachers should not wait for that to happen, because institutions do not change themselves. School boards, governments, universities, teacher federations, and other agencies will need to be pressured and persuaded to change.

Many recent trends and developments are now providing the right kinds of conditions and pressures for these changes to occur, but it will require concerted actions to bring them to fruition. Among these trends are the changing multicultural populations of our schools; distressing signs of persistent and increasing dropout and disaffection with school as the student proceeds higher up the system; limited impact of isolated reform strategies in such things as curriculum packages and inservice training; renewal of large proportions of the teaching force as older staff move through and out of the system; and the emergence of alternative forms of leadership, as more women move into administrative positions. Teachers themselves can add a lot to this pressure and persuasion. Favourable conditions, already exist. Alone and together, teachers can ignite the spark that will set it alight. Conditions always have to be right for change, but they have scarcely been "more right" than now. Teachers need to make the vital effort to exploit this opportunity. This is their individual and collective responsibility.

Individual responsibility means that "every action generates consequences the actor will eventually face" (Naisbitt and Aberdene, 1990: 298). Each individual is responsible for what he or she does, but not in isolation: "individuals seek community, avoiders of responsibility too often hide in the collective" (Naisbitt and Aberdene, 1990: 300).

Across the world today, we see people profoundly dissatisfied with the institutions which dominate their lives, and teachers should be dissatisfied with their schools and their systems. It may take only a few timely sparks to create the momentum for radical change. What is needed is for teachers and their principals to show the courage and commitment to ignite those vital sparks and to make the personal changes that will set in motion and contribute to institutional change. There are enough examples of developments along these lines already in evidence to predict that individuals and small groups can soon intersect with like-minded others to create ever increasing pockets of power. Administrators should be looking for and supporting these kinds of positive pressure points in helping to bring about reforms in institutions.

Collaborative cultures "lie within the control of those who participate in them; teachers and members together make their own schools" (Nias et al. 1989: 186). Teachers and principals can start in their own schools. Educators at all stages of their careers have a responsibility to act—beginning teachers to add new ideas and energies to the profession, and to avoid succumbing to the stale breath of routine; mid-career teachers to get out of the doldrums; and veteran teachers to pass on wisdom instead of cynicism. All have a responsibility to shape the schools of the future so that they are more productive and satisfying places to have a career as a teacher and to be a student.

It will not be enough to stop at the school level, however, because such cultures are too easily contained and destroyed over time. School districts must also work at nurturing and supporting collaborative schools, if they are to thrive. At the same time, interactive professionalism must be laced with cross-school and extra-district contact. While the school is the primary focus of collaboration, it is the profession of teaching as a whole that must be changed.

Teaching will always be a draining job. Teachers are involved in hundreds of interactions every day in potentially tension-filled circumstances. Anytime you have close contact day after day with large numbers of children in today's complex society, it will challenge the most energetic among us. But there are two types of exhaustion. One arises from lonely battles, unappreciated efforts, losing ground, and a growing and gnawing feeling of hopelessness that you cannot make a difference. The other type of exhaustion is the kind of thorough tiredness that accompanies hard work as part of a team, a growing recognition that you are engaged in a struggle that is worth the effort, and a recognition that what you are doing makes a critical difference for a recalcitrant child or a discouraged colleague. The former type of exhaustion ineluctably takes its toll on the motivation of the most enthusiastic teacher; the latter has its own inner reserve that allows us to bounce back after a good night's sleep. Indeed, the first type of exhaustion causes anxiety and sleeplessness, while the second induces rest and regeneration of energy.

School cultures make a difference in what kind of tiredness we experience. Will it be a thankless or a worthwhile expenditure of effort? It is up to each of us. Local administrators can and should help. But, the solution does not rest here alone. It is individuals and small groups of teachers and principals who must create the school and professional culture they want. This is what's worth fighting for—inside and outside your school.

**It is individuals and small groups of teachers and principals who must create the school and professional culture they want.**

# BIBLIOGRAPHY

Acker, S. (1989) *"It's what we do already, but . . .": Primary School Teachers and the 1988 Education Act,* Paper presented to conference on Ethnography, Education and Policy, St. Hilda's College, Oxford, September 1989.

Apple, M. W., and Jungck, S. (1991) "You don't have to be a teacher to teach in this unit: Teaching, technology and control in the classroom," in Hargreaves, A., and Fullan, M. (Eds) *Understanding Teacher Development,* London: Cassell.

Ashton, P., and Webb, R. (1986) *Making a Difference: Teachers' Sense of Efficacy and Student Achievement,* New York: Longman.

Ball, S. (1987) *The Micropolitics of the School,* London: Methuen.

Barth, R. (1990) *Improving Schools from Within: Teachers, Parents, and Principals Can Make the Difference,* San Francisco: Jossey-Bass.

Bennett, C. (1985) "Paints, pots or promotion? Art teachers' attitudes towards their careers," in Ball, S., and Goodson, I., *Teachers' Lives and Careers,* Philadelphia: Falmer Press.

Block, P. (1987) *The Empowered Manager,* San Francisco: Jossey-Bass.

Bolman, L., and Deal, T. (1990) *Reframing Organizations,* San Francisco: Jossey-Bass.

Coleman, P., and LaRocque, L. (1990) *Struggling To Be Good Enough: Administrative Practice and School District Ethos,* Lewes, UK: Falmer Press.

Connelly, F. M., and Clandinin, D. J. (1988) *Teachers As Curriculum Planners: Narratives of Experience,* New York: Teachers College Press.

Deal, T., and Kennedy, A. (1982) *Corporate Cultures,* Reading, MA: Addison-Wesley.

Deal, T., and Peterson, K. (1987) *Symbolic leadership and the school principal: Shaping school cultures in different contexts,* Unpublished paper, Vanderbilt University.

Flinders, D. J. (1988) "Teacher isolation and the new reform," *Journal of Curriculum and Supervision, 4*(1), pp. 17–29.

Fullan, M. (1988) *What's Worth Fighting For in the Principalship?: Strategies for Taking Charge in the Elementary School Principalship,* Toronto: Ontario Public School Teachers' Federation.

Fullan, M. (1990) "Staff development, innovation and institutional development," in Joyce, B. (Ed) *Changing School Culture Through Staff Development* (pp. 3–25), Alexandria, VA: Association for Supervision and Curriculum Development.

Fullan, M. (1991) *The New Meaning of Educational Change,* with S. Stiegelbauer, New York: Teachers College Press; Toronto: OISE Press, London: Cassell.

Fullan, M. (1993). *Change Forces,* Bristol, PA: Falmer Press, Taylor-Francis.

Fullan, M., Bennett, B., and Rolheiser-Bennett, C. (1990) "Linking classroom and school improvement," *Educational Leadership, 47*(8), pp. 13–19.

Fullan, M., Connelly, M., and Watson (1990) *Teacher Education in Ontario: Current Practices and Options for the Future,* Toronto: Ontario Ministries of Colleges and Universities and of Education.

Giddens, A. (1990) *The Consequences of Modernity,* Oxford: Polity Press.

Gilligan, C. (1982) *In a Different Voice: Psychological Theory and Women's Development,* Cambridge: Harvard University Press.

Goodson, I. (1991) "Sponsoring the teacher's voice: Teachers lives and teacher development," in Hargreaves, A., and Fullan, M. (Eds) *Understanding Teacher Development,* London: Cassell.

Grimmett, P., and Crehan, E. P. (1991) "The nature of collegiality in teacher development: The case of clinical supervision," in Fullan, M., and Hargreaves, A. (Eds) *Teacher Development and Educational Change,* Lewes: Falmer Press.

Grimmett, P., and Erickson, G. L. (Eds) (1988) *Reflection in Teacher Education,* New York: Teachers College Press.

Hargreaves, A. (1986) *Two Cultures of Schooling: The Case of Middle Schools,* Lewes: Falmer Press.

Hargreaves, A. (1989) *Curriculum and Assessment Reform,* Milton Keynes, United Kingdom: Open University Press.

Hargreaves, A. (1994) *Changing Teachers, Changing Times: Teachers' Work and Culture in the Postmodern Age,* New York: Teachers College Press.

Hargreaves, A., and Dawe, R. (1990) "Paths of professional development: Contrived collegiality, collaborative cultures, and the case of peer coaching," in *Teaching and Teacher Education, 6*(3), pp. 227–241.

Hargreaves, A., and Earl, L. (1990) *Rights of Passage,* Toronto: Ontario Ministry of Education.

Hargreaves, A., and Wignall, R. (1989) *Time for the Teacher: A Study of Collegial Relations and Preparation Time Use,* Toronto: Ontario Institute for Studies in Education.

Hart, A., and Murphy, M. (1990) "New teachers react to redesigned teacher work," *American Journal of Education, 98*(3), pp. 224–250.

Hickcox, E., Lawton, S., Leithwood, K., and Musella, D. (1988) *Making a Difference Through Performance Appraisal,* Toronto: OISE Press.

Huberman, M. (1988) "Teacher careers and school improvement," *Journal of Curriculum Studies, 20*(2), pp. 119–32.

Huberman, M. (1990) *The social context of instruction in schools,* Paper presented at American Educational Research Association annual meeting, Boston, Mass.

Huberman, M. (1991) "Teacher development and instructional mastery," in Hargreaves, A., and Fullan M. (Eds) *Understanding Teacher Development,* London: Cassell.

Hunt, D. (1987) *Beginning with Ourselves,* Toronto: OISE Press.

Hunt, D. (forthcoming) *The Personal Renewal of Energy,* Toronto: OISE Press.

Jackson, P. (1968) *Life in Classrooms,* New York: Holt, Rinehart and Winston.

Joyce, B., and Showers, B. (1988) *Student Achievement Through Staff Development,* New York: Longman.

Joyce, B., Murphy, C., Showers, B., and Murphy, J. (1989) "School renewal as cultural change," *Educational Leadership, 47*(3), pp. 70–8.

Kemmis, S., and McTaggart, R. (1988) *The Action Research Planner*, Deakin, Australia: University Press.

Krupp, J. A. (1989) "Staff development and the individual," in Caldwell, S. D. (Ed) *Staff Development: A Handbook of Effective Practices* (pp. 44–57), Oxford, OH: National Staff Development Council

Landsberg, M. (1990) *Education 2000*, Toronto: Toronto Teachers' Federation.

Leithwood, K. (1990) "The principal's role in teacher development," in Joyce, B. (Ed) *Changing School Culture Through Staff Development* (pp. 71–90), Virginia: ASCD.

Leithwood, K., and Jantzi, D. (1990) *Transformational leadership: How principals can help reform school culture*, Paper presented at American Educational Research Association annual meeting.

Leithwood, K., Dart, B., Jantzi, D., and Steinbach, R. (1990) *Implementing the Primary Program: The First Year*, British Columbia: B.C. Ministry of Education.

Lessing, D. (1986) *Prisons We Choose To Live Inside*, Toronto: CBC Enterprises.

Levine, D., and Eubanks, E. (1989) *Site-based management: Engine for reform or pipedream?* Unpublished manuscript.

Lieberman, A., and Miller, L. (1990) "Teacher development in professional practice and school," *Teachers College Record, 92*, pp. 105–22.

Little, J. W. (1981) "The power of organizational setting" (Paper adapted from final report, *School Success and Staff Development)*, Washington, DC: National Institute of Education.

Little, J. W. (1987) "Teachers as colleagues," in Richardson-Koehler, V. (Ed) *Educators' Handbook*, pp. 491–518, White Plains: Longman.

Little, J. W. (1990) "The persistence of privacy: Autonomy and initiative in teachers' professional relations," *Teachers College Record, 91*(4), pp. 509–36.

Lortie, D. (1975) *School Teacher: A Sociological Study*, Chicago: University of Chicago Press.

Louden, W. (1991) *Understanding Teaching*, London: Cassell.

Louis, K., and Miles, M. B. (1990) *Improving the Urban High School: What Works and Why*, New York: Teachers College Press.

Lytle, S., and Cochran-Smith, M. (1990) "Learning from teacher research: A working typology," *Teachers College Record, 92*(1), pp. 83–103.

McTaggart, R. (1989) "Bureaucratic rationality and the self-educating profession: The problem of teacher privatism," *Journal of Curriculum Studies, 2*(4), pp. 345–61.

Mortimore, P., Sammons, P., Stoll, L., Lewis, D., and Ecob, R. (1988) *School Matters: The Junior Years*, Somerset, United Kingdom: Open Books.

Naisbitt, J., and Aberdene, P. (1990) *Megatrends 2000*, New York: William Morrow.

Nias, J., Southworth, G., and Yeomans, R. (1989) *Staff Relationships in the Primary School*, London: Cassell.

Oberg, A., and Underwood, S. (1991) "Facilitating teacher development: Reflections on experience," in Hargreaves, A., and Fullan, M. (Eds) *Understanding Teacher Development*, London: Cassell.

Oja, S. N., and Smulyan, L. (1989) *Collaborative Action Research: A Developmental Approach*, Philadelphia: Falmer Press.

Peters, T. (1987) *Thriving on Chaos: Handbook for a Management Revolution*, New York: A. Knopf.

Pink, W. T. (1989) *Effective staff development for urban school improvement,* Paper presented at American Educational Research Association annual meeting.

Raymond, D., Butt, R., and Townsend, D. (1991) "Contexts for teacher development: Insights from teachers' stories," in Hargreaves, A., and Fullan, M. (Eds) *Understanding Teacher Development,* London: Cassell.

Richardson, V., and Anders, P. (1990) *The role of theory in descriptions of classroom reading practices,* Paper presented at American Educational Research Association annual meeting.

Robertson, H. J. (1991) "Teacher development and sex equity," in Hargreaves, A., and Fullan, M. (Eds) *Understanding Teacher Development,* London: Cassell.

Rosenholtz, S. (1989) *Teachers' Workplace: The Social Organization of Schools,* New York: Longman.

Ross, J., and Reagan, E. (1990) "Self-reported strategies of experienced and inexperienced curriculum consultants," *The Alberta Journal of Educational Research, 36*(2), 157–80.

Rothschild, J. (1990) *Feminist values and the democratic management of work organizations,* Paper presented at the 12th World Congress of Sociology, Madrid.

Rudduck, J. (1991) *Innovation and Change,* Milton Keynes: Open University Press.

Sarason, S. (1982) *The Culture of the School and the Problem of Change* (2nd ed.), Boston: Allyn and Bacon.

Sarason, S. (1990) *The Predictable Failure of Educational Reform,* San Francisco: Jossey-Bass.

Schön, D. (1987) *Educating the Reflective Practitioner,* San Francisco: Jossey-Bass.

Shakeshaft, C. (1987) *Women in Educational Administration,* Beverly Hills, CA: Sage.

Sikes, P. (1985) "The lifecycle of the teacher," in Ball, S., and Goodson, I., *Teachers' Lives and Careers,* Philadelphia: Falmer Press.

Sirotnik, K. A. (1987) *The School As the Center of Change* (Occasional Paper No. 5), Seattle, WA: Center for Educational Renewal.

Sizer, T. (1984) *Horace's Compromise,* Boston: Houghton-Mifflin.

Smith, W.F., and Andrews, R. L. (1989) *Instructional Leadership: How Principals Make a Difference,* Alexandria, VA: Association for Supervision and Curriculum Development.

Smyth, J. (1989) "A 'pedagogical' and 'educative' view of leadership," in Smyth, J. (Ed) *Critical Perspectives on Educational Leadership,* Lewes: Falmer Press.

Storr, A. (1988) *Solitude,* London: Flamingo Press.

Thiessen, D. (1991) "Classroom based teacher development," in Hargreaves, A., and Fullan, M. (Eds) *Understanding Teacher Development,* London: Cassell.

Tye, K. (1985) *The Junior High Schools in Search of a Mission,* Lanham: University Press of America.

Watson, N., and Kilcher, A. (1990) *Peer Coaching,* Toronto: Ontario Secondary School Teachers' Federation.

# ABOUT THE AUTHORS

**Michael Fullan** is the Dean of the newly formed Ontario Institute for Studies in Education of the University of Toronto. An innovator and leader in teacher education, he has developed a number of partnerships designed to bring about major school improvement and educational reform. He participates as researcher, consultant, trainer, and policy advisor on a wide range of educational change projects with school systems, teachers' federations, research and development institutes, and government agencies in Canada and internationally. In June 1990, as the first recipient of the Canadian Association of Teacher Educators (CATE) Award of Excellence, he was recognized for "outstanding contribution to his profession and to teacher education" and was seen as a "researcher/scholar practitioner of the highest caliber" by that organization. The Ontario Association of Curriculum Development awarded him the prestigious Colonel Watson Award for outstanding leadership in May 1993. In February 1995 he was appointed Policy Implementation Advisor to the Ministry of Education and Training regarding their response to the Royal Commission on Learning Report. He received the "Contribution to Staff Development" award in 1995 from the National Staff Development Council.

He has published widely on the topic of educational reform including *Change Forces* (Falmer Press), *The New Meaning of Educational Change* (Teachers College Press), and the *What's Worth Fighting For?* Series (Ontario Public School Teachers' Federation and Teachers College Press).

**Andy Hargreaves** is Director of and Professor in the International Centre for Educational Change at the Ontario Institute for Studies in Education. Before moving to North America in 1987, he taught primary school and lectured in several English universities. He is widely involved in consultation, research and improvement activities with teacher unions, universities, school districts, education ministries and Charitable Foundations across the world, and has held visiting professorships in England, Australia,

Sweden, Spain, and Japan. He is in high demand among these groups as a dynamic and motivational keynote speaker and workshop leader.

The author and editor of more than twenty books and monographs in education, he has established an international reputation as a leading authority and innovative thinker in the fields of teacher development, the culture of the school and educational reform. His book *Changing Teachers, Changing Times* received the 1995 Outstanding Writing Award from the American Association of Colleges for Teacher Education. Among his other recent books are *Schooling for Change* (with Lorna Earl and Jim Ryan) and *Teachers' Professional Lives* (edited with Ivor Goodson). He is also the invited editor of the 1997 ASCD Yearbook, *Positive Change for School Success*.